BEYOND NEGATIVE ETHNICITY, CORRUPTION AND VIOLENCE:
In Salvage of Africa's Soul

Wanjohi Kibicho, Ph.D.

SAKATA
Publishers

Ottawa ♦ London

Copyright © 2019 Wanjohi Kibicho, Ph.D.

Apart from any fair dealing for the purpose of research or private study, or criticism or review, as permitted under the Copyright, Designs and Patents Act 1988, this publication may only be reproduced, stored or transmitted, in any form or by any means, with prior permission in writing of the copyright owner. Enquiries concerning reproduction outside these terms should be sent to the publisher at the undermentioned address:

228 Millroad Way
Ottawa, ON
K1E 2C9
CANADA

Published by Sakata Publishers
Ottawa, Canada 2019

A catalogue record for this book is available from the Library and Archives of Canada
ISBN-978-1-9991291-0-1
ISBN- 978-1-9991291-1-8 (e-book)

Cover designed by Wesley Naftie & Serena Fancy
Typeset by Karen Sephora
Printed and bound by Lulu Press, Morrisville, North Carolina, USA

Dedication

To
My mother: Sephora.
Who rais'd me to belie'e in fairness;
And, justice for all.
To belie'e in the potential of all people.

To
My brother: David Senior.
Who was called home at the nascent stage of this project.
Your life reminds us that, time's like a river.
You can't touch the same water twice.
Because the flow that has pass'd will ne'er pass again.
Live your life to the fullest.

To
My stars: Karen, Wesley 'n Serena.
For, in your presence,
E'eryday brings a fresh-start.
And, your happiness reinforces my resolve;
Makin' my life whole.

To
My idols: non-ethnic chauvinists, dead or alive.
Your lives are a testimony that,
We're tied together in network of mutuality.
Towards a common destiny.
For, I can ne'er be what I ought to be;
Till you're what you ought to be.

Acknowledgement

Every book is the product of inspirations and collaborations across spatial-temporal continuum. Thus, many individuals helped me to gather materials for this book, and each cannot be singled-out for thanks. Some I have mentioned here; of many others I must ask that they take this book itself as a testimony of my gratitude and as a witness to the fact that their effort was not (entirely) wasted.

Foremost I owe an overwhelming debt of gratitude to my model - President Nelson Mandela (1918-2013). Every single moment I hear your soothing voice telling me: *do not love; be love*. My brief but intense association with you will forever remain indelibly etched on my personality.

To my esteemed teachers: Plato (424-347 BC), Aristotle (384-322 BC), Seneca (4 BC-65 AD), Miyamoto Musashi (1584-1645), Gichin Funakoshi (1868-1957) and Morihei Ueshiba (1883-1969). Your philosophical writings profoundly changed my dealings with fellow beings. You collectively taught me: *it comes from within...*

My sincere acknowledgement to the many interviewees, who allowed me to intrude on their time and privacy so that I could collect their stories. All names, unless otherwise stated, are pseudonyms only aimed at concealing personal identities of the respondents.

Friends and colleagues have given me much exacting and practical assistance by reading some parts of this text as it progressed. Particular acknowledgment goes to Jane Dyer (UK), Kiragu Wangai (USA) and Judy Hersey (Canada) who rooted-out numerous infelicities of style and unclear nuances of meaning. A special mention goes to the anonymous reviewer, for her critical comments on an early draft of the manuscript. Thanks to you all for taking time to deeply engage with my scholarship. Similarly, I extend deep thanks to Jullie LeBlanc, who efficiently transcribed all the tapes. I am deeply indebted to Maria Ostrovskaya for her excellent cartographic work; and, to George Bojedomov for the outstanding cover picture. To you all, I greatly appreciate your insights and time.

A word of thanks to my consistent supporters and friends: James Mbogo (Moo), Cédric Beng, Simon Kagia, Wilda Ombongi, Anthony Karia, Richard Ndivo, Elijah Kasati, Christine Mutua, Samson Obiya, Rajabu Mtunge, Milka Wambui, James Ndung'u, Amos Chore, Elizabeth Muvuli, Charles Lange, Martha Khasiali, Francis Karani, Nora Mutai, Alex Gichira, Oliver Mukunza, Lincoln Amwayi, Moses Maina, Patrick Ngondi, Gideon Akwabi, John Jones, Beatrice Njeri, Shirllynn Valai, Bernard Mbire, Rose Arusei, Isabella Mapelu, Troy Messam, and George Mugendi. Your company through variegated social media platforms made the compiling of this book less stressful. Your warm hearts make the world a better place to live in. For, it is not the size of the candle that matters, but the intensity of its light.

Appreciations also go to Richard DeLisle, Stephanie Kalt, Tracy Pressé, Nicole Perras, Paul Harris, Tracy Brown, Patrick Kennedy, Diane Brulé, Jack Wilson, and Tracy Henderson. You are like a candle that consumes itself to light the way to others.

And, finally, with great affection, I acknowledge my family, broadly defined, who are my core support team and a source of comfort and pleasure: Naftie (late), Leah (late), Sephora, Grace (mom), Beatrice, James, Jackson, Emily, Pauline, John, Evelyn,

Michael, Mary, Nelly, David Senior (late), Hillary (late), Susan, William, David Junior, Jefither, Peter, Ann, Peninna, Edna, Presley, Julian, Bernard, Caroline, Duncan, Grace and Paul. I can never thank you enough for without your love, kindness and enduring faith in me, I would not be the person I am today. You all shaped my philosophical way of looking at the world. No matter what I do in the balance of my life, I will always cherish you in my heart. For, you are a part of me.

Errors of facts, judgment and interpretation that remain in this book are solely mine.

Personal note

The issues motivating the *Beyond Negative Ethnicity, Corruption and Violence: In Salvage of Africa's Soul* journey are both philosophical and behavioural, and I come at them from my professional background in these disciplines. Further, it is shaped by my realization that all human beings move in the same direction and towards the same goal – pursuit of happiness. This realization is based on my intense interactions with the citizens of the world as I undertook varied types of social science studies. However, *Beyond Negative Ethnicity, Corruption and Violence* is intended for the general audience. Anyone who intends to enrich his life by experiencing the art of love can hope to find something uplifting by reading this book.

Gathering and processing the information represented in this book has both broadened and deepened my love for Africa. It is my sincere hope that this collection of wisdom will do the same for you dear reader.

All proceeds from the sale of this book go to charity in support of the underprivileged children in Africa. In which case, I thank you for buying a copy of this book, as it will have a direct positive effect on a poor and deprived child's wellbeing on this earth.

Most importantly, you not only bought the book, but you are reading it. Do not be like the fifteen percent of people who buy books but never read past the first chapter. Read and use this book's lessons to produce tangible results in both your life and the lives of those around you.

Before you skip the rest of this sentimental commentary and go on to the meat of this book, let me tell you that many of my readers ask me why I donate the proceeds of all my books to charity. The response is: I give because I learnt to give. Not because I have plenty, but because I know how it feels to have nothing. And, no one has ever become poor by giving. Furthermore, genuine charity is not an obligation; it is an opportunity to give back. So do not look for heroes; be one! You do not have to be a Nelson Mandela - although you could, if you desired! Remember though:

Life is a balance

Life is a balance between givin' 'n receivin';
Between takin' care of self;
And, takin' care of others.
Between givin' to those in need;
And, givin' to self.
Do so with joy 'n guilt-free.

Take not the world's weight on your shoulders.
Just do your little bit.
See someone in trouble,
Make him feel lov'd.
Touch him in a new way.
Empower him.
And, your contribution becomes a pleasure;
Not a burden!

Finally, I have to confess that I am a little afraid to suggest what I am going to suggest. But, I am more afraid not to - that we begin this journey, *Beyond Negative Ethnicity, Corruption and Violence,* joined together in a minute of silence in memory of all Africans who have lost their lives due to (political) violence.

Asante!
Dank je!
Grand merci!
Tremendous thanks!
Arigatō gozai-mashita!

Wanjohi Kibicho, Ph.D.
Ottawa, Canada,
June 2019

Prologue: Lesson from President Mandela

There is a club in life that you join unknowingly. I call it: *The Perspective-Changing Club*. The registration fee is payable in full, up-front for a life-time membership. The prime benefit of joining the club is a new found perspective on life, and a deep understanding of fellow beings.

As a cardinal rule, the club has no listing of its members, but affiliates are identifiable by a simple peek at their hearts. They are unreservedly counselled to exchange sporadic eye contacts with all those they deal with that say: *I love you*. Thus, it is easy to spot the club members from afar as they provide random acts of kindness and associate themselves with the down-trodden in society. They look for goodness in others, and treat them as if that's all they see. They spread hope and optimism; share love and joy; exude passion and compassion; and, fight for justice and fairness for all. As they rise by uplifting others.

I paid my dues; my life-time membership arrived back in May 2000 in Pretoria, South Africa, not by mail, but by a deep life-changing conversation that I had with President Nelson Mandela – See Appendix 2. He told me: *any form of violence is self-defeating and counterproductive. Be love.* To elucidate the foregoing, I share with you, dear reader, the humbling lesson that I learnt from this apartheid paragon. This will, I hope, aid you to engage in a helpful deconstruction of the discourse and counter-discourse presented herein.

Meeting with President Nelson Mandela

Together with a group of international scholars, I was given a rare opportunity to meet with President Mandela. As protocol dictates, we were asked to send our questions and/or areas of interest that we wanted Mr. Mandela to talk about a week before the meeting date. After reading Mr. Mandela's autobiography, *Long Walk to Freedom*, twice, I had difficulty fully grasping his explanation of his love for boxing as a sport – see page 193 of the noted book.

Consequently, I prepared a question asking him to help me understand his position, bearing in mind that he stood against all forms of violence throughout his life. I was excited that my question had been retained out of the many that we had submitted. He opened his narrative by asking me: *are you a boxer my dear friend? No, but I am an ardent martial artist,* I responded. Then, he continued:

> It is true; boxing gave me pleasure and satisfaction. However, I never enjoyed the violence associated with it as any form of violence is self-defeating and counterproductive. Even when it appears like violence is doing good, that goodness is only temporary while the damage it causes is permanent. Nevertheless, I liked the fact that boxing is egalitarian. While in the ring, all participants are equal. Their socio-economic standing, beliefs, level of education, age, gender, sex-orientation and race, among others, are irrelevant.

> Related to this point, any organized sport can create hope where there is only despair. It has the necessary power to break down human-generated barriers as it laughs in the face of all types of hatreds. It creates genuine love (see also Kibicho 2016: 77-78).

President Mandela asked us to go beyond *loving* and *be love*. He instructed us to be love that rains on the saints and the sinners. Love that shines on the good and the bad alike. For, the good is half-bad; and, the bad is half-good. And, the light cannot exist in the absence of darkness; as the day is undefinable without the night. It is by means of opposites that eternity endures. He reminded us:

…Never says…

A rose ne'er says:
I'll give my fragrance to the virtuous people;
But withhold it from the vicious ones.

A lamp ne'er says:
I'll give my light to the righteous souls;
But withhold it from the evil ones.

A tree ne'er says:
I'll give my shade to the good guys;
But withhold it from the nasty ones.

These are the images of what to *be love* is. Immediately thereafter, I summarised the meeting in the following words:

For the love of humanity, have no moral middle ground and refuse indifference as an option to violence. Be unyielding and inflexible in its opposition. Be intelligent. Be loving. Be caring. Be grateful. Make a difference.

I wrote these words on the front page of my pocket notebook that I have carried religiously ever since. [Spoiler alert: I will shamelessly repeat this *Life Lesson* throughout the balance of this book as it greatly inspires me whenever faced by unfair and unjust situations. Hopefully, it will do the same for you dear reader.] For, at Mandela's smile, I smiled.

Mandela: at your smile, I smiled

What an honour!
Meetin' the Master of the art-of-love.
What a privilege!
Residin' in the world famous Museum of Apartheid!
Under the angelic wings,
Of the Paragon of the art-of-peace 'n forgi'eness.
The Exemplar of the art-of-reconciliation 'n togetherness.
President Nelson Mandela!

O' Mandela!
At your smile, I smil'd;
And, into my soul there came an exquisite ray-of-love!
My soul was bow'd,
In the depths of humility.
You told me;
Love 'n forgi'eness are constructi'e.
Hatred 'n bitterness are destructi'e.
And, the secret of the greatest enjoyment of being is:
To be love!

O' Madiba!
I'll ne'er dishonour your teachings.
Ne'er will I contaminate your actionable view of love.
For, with it, you usher'd in light,
When dark clouds approach'd:
Drivin' away hatred;
Unifyin' the oppress'd 'n the oppressors.

Let's talk 'n walk Madiba's language.
Language of peace 'n forgi'eness;
Reconciliation 'n togetherness.
Language of belie'e 'n hope;
Patience 'n love.

Table of Contents

Dedication I
Acknowledgement III
Prologue: Lesson from President Mandela IX
Table of Contents XIII
Setting the Scene of Exploration 1
Ethnic Chauvinism: War Minus Gunshots 17
Equal Opportunities: Antidote to Social Exclusion 31
Economic, Social and Political Corruption 41
In Violence, Humanity Loses 61
Domestic Violence: The Frontline of War Against Humanity 73
Political Violence in Africa 95
Good Leadership: Extraction of Innate Greatness 113
Love: The Mother of All Virtues 123
Failure: A Stepping Stone to Success 135
Be Grateful of Who You Are 147
Thank You Dear Reader: Concluding Remarks 157
References 169
Appendices 171

CHAPTER 1

Setting the Scene of Exploration

Africa: Rhythm of love, peace and joy

Africa's love.
So says her stunnin' valleys.
Where magnificent rivers flow life.
Under the proud eye of birds-of-the-sky.

Africa's peace.
So says her splendid savannah.
Where lions caress her skin.
With elegancy glitterin' their pride.

Africa's joy.
So says her lofty mountains.
Where monkeys swin' tree-to-tree.
With majestic delight of cliffs 'n peaks.

Africa's unity.
So says her virtuous cultures.
Where hearts palpitate in a unifi'd rhythm.
Rhythm of love, peace 'n joy.

Africa's future.
So says her turquoise sea.
Where jewel fishes sing her praise.
As the water washes her feet in re'erence.

Preamble

Many aspects of African societies are marred by prejudice that begets negative ethnicity; malfeasance that engenders corruption; and, intolerance that spawns violence of varying forms. Together, these social ills make the trail leading to Africa's optimal destination treacherous. The intensity and constancy of these challenges leave many people wondering:

(i) How and when did the continent start this downward spiral?
(ii) Will the continent ever get back to the righteous trajectory?
(iii) What can individual Africans do to redeem the existent conditions?

Answering these three questions is the primary focus of this book. Undoubtedly, these answers will provide keys to the city of hope, which has the potential to shape the continent's shared destiny. Thus, to answer them, I dissected the soul of modernity. In the process, I realized that the primary cause of all manner of sufferings in Africa is barren minds. Minds totally blinded by the after-life – the need to go to heaven. Inversely, one does not need to be a genius to realize that the emphasis on heaven and hell is a distraction; it begets followers who live their lives talking and walking, while their minds slept. To be at peace with their transgressions to fellow humans, they make the 'heaven's-keeper' a shareholder in their misdeeds by occupying the front seats in the places of worship.

The way-out of this social conundrum is a simple mind change. A change I refer to as silent social revolution. A revolution based on awareness towards the fulfilment of individual potential. This revolution only requires brains, higher vision and profound thoughts; but, no physical strength and no harming another being. This realization and the need to (re)activate enlightenment in all was the seed of the *Beyond Negative Ethnicity, Corruption and Violence*. Consequently, this book is not a treatise to seek sympathy, nor an attempt to reach heaven, but an essential and practical service towards humanity.

Therefore, it is with great respect that I open my heart in this congenial relationship with you as together, we embark on this journey code-named: *Beyond Negative Ethnicity, Corruption and Violence*. A journey of facing our reality head-on and together forging actionable strategies. As life is a gift, it offers us the privilege, opportunity, and responsibility to give something back by becoming more. Therefore, I begin our journey by detailing the trail that will lead us to our destination by setting-out the scene of our exploration.

Nonetheless, if you are like me, to really understand what is going on in Africa, you need a proem that involves swordfights, weird monsters and people getting thrown off castle walls. So, here you go...

The Fortress in a Seemingly Peaceful World

Once upon a time... There was a *Fortress in a Seemingly Peaceful Realm*. This *Fortress* is a living, breathing presence, unimpressed by what others say is impossible, proud of its own success, generous, sometimes wrong but always eager to provide a better life for its citizens in a framework of justice, fairness and freedom.

Unfortunately, the *Fortress* struggles with determined devilish creatures. Every season, *the War Council* meets to try and foresee future enemy attacks. Using sophisticated prediction methodologies, *the War Council* identifies all the threatening creatures.

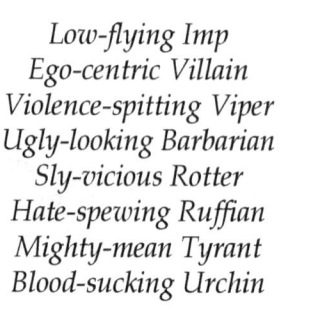

Low-flying Imp
Ego-centric Villain
Violence-spitting Viper
Ugly-looking Barbarian
Sly-vicious Rotter
Hate-spewing Ruffian
Mighty-mean Tyrant
Blood-sucking Urchin

Then, *the War Council* lists the enemies in order of priority, starting with the most vicious to the least barbarous. Because of scarce resources however, the number of beasts to be dealt with must be limited. So, each season, *the War Council* has unbendable instructions to focus on two quintessential factors:

- ❖ The enemies that are most likely to attack the Dominion in the coming season; and,
- ❖ The most atrocious adversaries.

The top-three enemies

Out of the long list therefore, *the War Council* has to settle on the top-three of the incontestable bad guys. After lengthy deliberations, *the Council* settled on: *The Hate-spewing Ruffians*, *The Blood-sucking Urchins* and *The Violence-spitting Vipers*. Then, it studied them in-depth in order to match them with the best type of warriors in *the Fortress in a Seemingly Peaceful Realm*. Consequently, *the War Council* described the enemies as follows.

The Hate-spewing Ruffians subscribe to both liberal and conservative ideologies. As such, they are not confined to a particular political divide, as their unifying characteristic is propagation of prejudice through blatant hypocrisy coated by undemocratic practices. They have a high blood pressure of chauvinistic words and anaemia of destructive acts. Hatred is the trademark of their profession as they find fictitious faults in those who do not resemble them and then maltreat them for it. For they have shrunk so far into darkness that objects in bright daylight appear blurred. Their souls are dazed and befogged, envious of the blind! Thence, they receive an injury by way of excuse to do one themselves. They are egomaniacs.

The Blood-sucking Urchins also lie within the entire political spectrum. They tear from place to place and unsettle themselves with one move after another, which is symptomatic of ill minds. They are reactionary guardians of the status quo who draw public revenue like some demonic, destructive suction tubes. With their bodies stuffed full and minds wholly starved, they induce vomit to empty their stomachs for more. They loath anyone who comes between them and public coffers. Further, they have devised creative ways to disguise their self-serving deeds with altruism. At their core however, they are ultra-selfish.

The Violence-spitting Vipers look sympathetically at all political views such that they fail to be committed to either side. Their political stand changes depending on who is able and willing to pay for their evil deeds. They are apt to be robbed of their senses by mere passing fancies, to the point where their anger is called out by anything that fails to answer to their will. For, they are tyrants who have perfected the art of destroying the two most cherished African institutions: family and community. They leave their victims with nothing to build on, save bitterness and hopelessness. They are senseless dimwits.

The War Council summarises its finding as follows: the three enemies are close-minded, short-sighted, self-seeking and overly committed to injustice. They have a degenerative spirit, which sees nothing right in the way the universe is ordered, and would rather reform the immortal gods than reform themselves. They are like the barren sandy ground of the Sahara desert, which sucks in all the rain with greediness, but yields no fruitful plants for the benefit of others. In brief terms, they are excellent surrogates for those who tell hard-working, forward-thinking citizens: *slow down for a while; you are pushing too fast*. They spread their war by deliberately appealing to the deepest hate responses within the human heart.

The War Council therefore further observes: our only hope today lies in our ability to recapture the post-independence revolutionary spirit; and, go out into uncompromising mode and declare eternal hostility to these three goddesses of darkness. We need to go beyond negative ethnicity, corruption and violence. With such a powerful commitment, we shall boldly challenge the status quo to ensure that the crooked areas are straightened while the rough edges are smoothened. For this to materialize, we must embrace a wide ranging fellowship that lifts neighbourly concern beyond our ethnic cocoons.

Based on these findings, *the War Council* identifies the three best-suited warriors to deal with the three foes: *the Lance-launching Cavalry; the Arch-shooting Squadron*; and, *the Waterball-slinging Platoon*. Specifically, *the Lance-launching Cavalry* is assigned *The Hate-spewing Ruffians*; *the Arch-shooting Squadron* is matched with *The Blood-sucking Urchins* while *the Waterball-slinging Platoon* is paired with *The Violence-spitting Vipers*. As they assign these roles, the members of *the War Council* appreciates the fact that challenges posed by the three monsters are all tied together. They are triple evils that are interrelated and they should be approached as such.

Finally, the season when the attacks take place arrives. Then, the night falls, which is the most susceptible time of the period. Express directive is that all entry and exit points have to be manned by at least three mean-looking and well-equipped warriors: one from *the Lance-launching Cavalry*; another one from *the Arch-shooting Squadron*; and, the last one from *the Waterball-slinging Platoon*. As per the latest press release from *the War Council*, the troops are ready; and, strategically positioned at all vulnerable points of *the Fortress in a Seemingly Peaceful Realm*. Nevertheless, the situation on the ground is in conflict with the foregoing. For, the deployment of the troopers is amateurish and chaotic, leaving many sensitive areas ill protected or out-right unguarded.

In a typical attack season, the troops destroy between 31 to 36 percent of the bad guys. And, that is pretty good! Yes, good due to the fluid nature of these attacks: the chosen trio archenemies are highly unpredictable; their tactics are ever-changing while their weapons of choice are constantly evolving.

As if that is not enough, unprecedented surprise awaits the Kingdom's warriors this season. *The Hate-spewing Ruffians* have experienced a total transformation; and, now have multiple tongues and highly slippery bodies. Spears and arrows cannot touch them as they are easily deflected by their slimy bodies while waterballs caress their tongues. *The Blood-sucking Urchins* have metamorphosed; and, now are flying at a supersonic speed. Arrows and spears can no longer reach them, and waterballs quench their thirst. *The Violence-spitting Vipers* have undergone a mutation; and, are now in flames. Waterballs tickle them, then evaporate into thin air while any direct contact with arrows and spears energizes them before they melt off. Bottom line, it is total carnage in *the Fortress in a once Seemingly Peaceful Realm*!

After the overwhelming bloody defeat, *the War Council* convenes again to take stock. *The failure of our war strategy this season was impossible to predict* – the disoriented members unanimously conclude. *The War Council* nevertheless reminds the peace loving citizens that the season of attacks is not yet over, and that they need to remain alert, for the brutal creatures are still off the leash. Nonetheless, within the population, the vast majority cannot understand this failure due to the generous budget allocated to *the War Council*; and, the overplayed bravado on how well prepared *the Council* was to deal with any imminent attack.

For readers who find metaphors dull, here are some explanations:

- *The Fortress in a Seemingly Peaceful Realm* is the continent of Africa.
- *The War Council* is the Cabinet of any ruling government in Africa.
- 'Attack season' is any day of the year; 'night' is the electioneering year.
- *The Hate-spewing Ruffian* is negative ethnicity while *The Hate-spewing Ruffians* are ethnic chauvinists.
- *The Blood-sucking Urchin* is corruption of all kinds while *The Blood-sucking Urchins* are the corrupt individuals.
- *The Violence-spitting Viper* is violence of all forms while *The Violence-spitting Vipers* are violent individuals or propagators of violence.
- *The Lance-launching Cavalry* include: the Judiciary and the offices of the public prosecution in Africa.
- *The Arch-shooting Squadron* is the police services in the continent.
- *The Waterball-slinging Platoon* include: the anti-corruption commissions or bodies and the electoral commissions or bodies in Africa.

THE FORTRESS MUST SUBDUE THE THREE MONSTERS

Experts, read *the War Council*, believe that the three priority monsters have undergone mutation this season; but, maybe it was *the Lance-launching Cavalry, the Arch-shooting Squadron* and *the Waterball-slinging Platoon* who were ill-prepared. Who knows?

Nonetheless, there are those who would argue that *the Fortress in a Seemingly Peaceful Realm*, Africa, has reached the zenith of her power; that her people are weak and fearful, reduced to bickering with each other and no longer possess the will to cope with these challenges – *The Hate-spewing Ruffian* (negative ethnicity); *The Blood-sucking Urchin* (corruption); and, *The Violence-spitting Viper* (violence). They would like Africans to learn to live with these social problems – negative ethnicity, corruption and violence. They would love to see Africans teach their children that it is futile to dream; and, if they dare to dream, it is impossible to make those dreams a reality. I do not believe in that, and the pages that follow prove exactly that. I do not believe you do either. For you have decided to join me in this ambitious journey *Beyond Negative Ethnicity, Corruption and Violence*.

Together, I am convinced we shall, and we must, subdue these monsters: one part negative ethnicity; one part corruption; and, one part violence. United, they are a trial of Africa's spiritual resolve; the values citizens hold; the beliefs they cherish; and, the ideals to which they are dedicated. They test Africans' will and threaten the moral fibre of the very African-hood. Therefore, they are problems of flesh and blood as they cause untold pain and unparalleled destruction.

With able leadership, time, love and a little dose of hope, the forces of good will ultimately triumph over evil. Unquestioningly, optimism comes less easily in contemporary times, not because Africans are less vigorous, but because the known enemies have refined their instruments of repression. As a result, ethnic-linked hatred is omnipresent, socio-economic inequalities are on expansion and deep political rifts are widening. Though these challenges are fearsome, so are Africans' determination and abilities.

Beyond Negative Ethnicity, Corruption and Violence: In Salvage of Africa's Soul

I wrote *Beyond Negative Ethnicity, Corruption and Violence* for one reason: to be a wake-up call that will challenge all towards an all-inclusive, prosperous Africa. Therein are ideas and strategies to help you produce long-lasting changes in yourself and others. Its overarching goal is therefore, to bring people together; and, to give hope to future generations.

To talk about the future generation is to think forward. To move forward, Africans must learn from their history, without identifying it as a limit of their reality. For, you find yourself by living in the present and never by dwelling in the past. Only then shall Africans be able to forge their envisaged future. As you do so however, you need to focus on the journey, and not the destination, for joy is found in doing an activity not in finishing it. My teacher Morihei Ueshiba puts this better than I can do. He says: an artist derives more pleasure from painting than from having completed a picture. When his whole attention is absorbed in concentration on the work at hand, a tremendous sense of satisfaction is created in him by his very absorption. Once he lifts his hands off the finished piece, from then on what he is enjoying is the art's end product, whereas it was the art itself he was enjoying when painting. Thus, enjoy the journey.

Throughout the journey though, you need to give voices to the voiceless; and, imagine yourself into the lives of those who do not have your privileges. That said, here is a song for you dear reader.

Song for you

This is a song for you!
For, your face isn't deform'd by goodies of good-life;
Shout at the stars, 'n tell 'em to calm their loud twinklin'.
As the man of the dark desolate street wants to sleep.
So that he can finish what you start'd;
Then finish what he start'd.
Appreciate the trials 'n strain;
Recognize the sacrifices 'n efforts-in-vain;
And, understand the losses 'n pain...
Then, you'll judge his innate 'imperfections' with more patient charity.

O' you of undeform'd face!
Where the mind's muddl'd;
And, the thought's twist'd;
Straighten it with golden bits of kindness;
And, a little shake of love.
Cheer-up the singin' man of the dark desolate street.
Help him climb the life's pesky ladder;
And, you'll find your life-path amply wide for two.
For, only the heavy loads we help'd lighten'll count.

Once you help lighten the heavy load in the heart of *the singing man of the dark desolate street*, your existence will be celebrated beyond your families, as you will have positively influenced the reality of many. This is the only power that you need to have so as to vivify the entire humanity. You do not need to raise your hands to heaven. Equally, you do not need to implore the temple warden to allow you close to the ear of some graven image, as though this increases the chances of you being heard. Deity is near you; he is with you; he is within you. Look for him in your neighbour's heart, for that is where he resides.

In many instances, *Beyond Negative Ethnicity, Corruption and Violence* uses animals in stories and illustrations to dramatize and at the same time to detach human feelings from the ensuing discussion. And, for animals are instinctual and their emotions are simple and pure.

The *taijitu* symbol, *Yin-Yang*, used to usher a new *Section*, has a deep philosophical meaning. It implies that nothing is completely *Yin* (shaded side) or completely *Yang* (unshaded side). The *Yin* portion of the *Yin-Yang* contains a small amount of *Yang*, and in a similar manner, the *Yang* portion has a small amount of *Yin*. In other words, each aspect contains the beginning point for the other aspect. For example, day cannot exist without the night. In the presence of one, the other disappears. The two are interdependent upon each other and therefore the definition of one requires the definition for the other to be complete. The nature of *Yin* and *Yang* flows and changes with time. Using our *day-night* example, the day gradually flows into night. They are not static entities. In relation to this book, this symbol reminds us that human life cannot be absolute and static. For it to be relevant, *Yin* and *Yang* mutually aid and change each other for difficult and easy complement each other as they are both part of our daily lives. The interaction of the two establishes the much-needed harmony in life.

Both women and men are equally important in any society. I have therefore decided to use *he, his* and *himself* to represent both the feminine and masculine genders. They are only used in the interest of brevity and easy reading.

Although the book is divided into two unequally distributed Parts, its connections and teachings are nonlinear. These Parts overlap and amplify each other. Thus, **Part 1** introduces us into the challenges facing *the Fortress in a Seemingly Peaceful Realm*: negative ethnicity, corruption and violence. Overwhelmed by these social monsters, many Africans seem unable to distinguish right from left; right from wrong and light from darkness. Thus, the crooked seems straight while the unlawful seems lawful. Consequently, the socio-econo-political game is disorderly as players and/or the referees are unclear of what constitutes a foul. Rules are applied impartially and/or subjected to arbitrary changes. This leads to confusion; and, chaos is the order of the day in many aspects of life within *the Fortress*.

Finally, **Part 2** takes a different approach by creatively underscoring the fact that everyone in *the Fortress in a Seemingly Peaceful Realm* has a gift to contribute. Everyone has a role in the fight against the triple brutes of negative ethnicity, corruption and violence. Thus, this Part of the book calls upon Africans to look at the continent as a mosaic made up of numerous brilliantly coloured pieces. Pieces that complement, or should complement, each other. To thrive therefore, Africa needs everyone to contribute his unique gift(s). For a woman is not beautiful when her hair or abundant derrière wins compliments, but when her total appearance diverts admiration from the individual parts of her body.

Beyond Negative Ethnicity, Corruption and Violence is meant for anyone who believes in and strives for good living: fairness, justice and love. It is invaluable to: policy makers, opinion shapers, the media, social workers, police, development practitioners, members of the judiciary and anyone who is interested in understanding the dynamics of good living and how it impacts on daily lives in the continent.

Concluding remarks

Africans must listen to and take care of each other. For as a people, you cannot learn from one another until you stop screaming at each other; until you speak quietly enough so that your voice and words can be heard.

You must work and walk together; and, support and encourage one another. For abilities wither under fault-finding, blossom with encouragement. With encouragement, the daughter of a peasant farmer becomes a surgeon; and, the son of a street-hawker becomes a teacher. Once this happens:

You win!
Your neighbour wins!
Africa wins!
Humanity wins!
As you stand tall without standin' on another;
And, become a victor with no victim.

Nonetheless, the foregoing remains foggy due to omnipresent prejudice, which *begets negative ethnicity*. This brings us to the first phase, Part 1, of our journey *Beyond Negative Ethnicity, Corruption and Violence*.

PART 1

PREJUDICE BEGETS NEGATIVE ETHNICITY

Prejudice's the mother of negative ethnicity.
Negative ethnicity gives birth to ethnic chauvinists.
Who assume loud is strong 'n quiet's weak.
They curse darkness instead of lightin' a candle.
For, they're toxic.

Dear reader, avoid toxic people.
For, they'll manipulate you.
If they can't control you;
They'll influence how others see you.
By misinformin' them about you.
Misinformation'll feel unfair.
But, stay above it.
For, others'll e'entually see the truth;
Just like you did.

Dear ethnic chauvinist, as a goldsmith sifts dust from gold;
Remo'e your impurities - hatred.
Conquer your wild thoughts;
Tame your crude words 'n master your savage actions.
And, let love flourish.
For, *ethnic chauvinism is war minus gunshots.*

CHAPTER 2

Ethnic Chauvinism: War Minus Gunshots

Africa's pastime

Our continental pastime!
It's efficient.
Keeps itself in shape.
Efficiently tracks us down;
Then, rapidly pounces upon us.
For, it's unalike other pastimes,
It's negative ethnicity!

It gives birth to self.
Gives birth to the reasons that give it life.
When it sleeps…
Ne'er an eternal rest.
For, even sleeplessness saps not its strength;
It feeds it.
Gives it a runnin' start.
Till it attains a self-sustainin' momentum.

O' our continental pastime - negative ethnicity!
Has a scarr'd face twist'd in a grimace;
Of erotic ecstasy.
Numbs our reasonin' makin' us listless weaklings.
Addin' countless pages of our dark-history.
And, wea'ing unbound'd fugly human carpet-of-blood.

Oh yeah, our continental pastime tires not.
For, its leitmotif - the impeccable executioner;
Untirin' unimpeachable sniper.
Unflinchingly snipin' Africa's future.

Preamble

In diversity, one understands that what he believes to be real is still subjective and therefore not necessarily everyone's reality. Thus, to know what is inherently wrong, one needs to adopt a self-evident principle: an action is wrong when it is intended to cause harm to another being who is unwilling to participate in the harm; and, or has not initiated the harm. This argument is premised on the fact that human beings are not random creatures; they do everything for a reason. That reason might exist only unconsciously, but there is always a driving force behind any behaviour.

In line with the foregoing, scientific research shows that human behaviour is geared towards either avoidance of pain/suffering or generation of pleasure/happiness. In this process, an individual intentionally or unintentionally, knowingly or unknowingly induces pain or pleasure to those directly or indirectly affected by the behaviour in question.

Consequently, prejudice and negative ethnicity serve two purposes: to generate pleasure to the instigators; and, to induce pain to those on the receiving end. Either way though, negative ethnicity has irreparable consequences at all levels – individual, family, society, national as well as continental. This is the point of departure of the present chapter as it dissects the consequences of negative ethnicity currently devastating *the Fortress in a Seemingly Peaceful Realm* – Africa.

From social categorization to prejudice

The ever-changing world bombards us with an overwhelming amount of sensory stimulation. This makes it impossible for the human mind to interpret and respond to every event that it encounters. This is so because such stimuli possess many characteristics in common with each other, as well as attributes which distinguish them from one another. Yet, for survival-sake, nature requires human beings to detect occurrences, make reasonably accurate predictions about how they will affect them, and behave accordingly.

By assigning objects to categories based on their similarities and differences, humans acquire a considerable amount of information about them by simply recalling the defining features of the category. For example, trying to remember individual characteristics of twenty different animals in a national park might be a daunting task; but if fifteen of them fit the category of 'zebras' and the remaining five fit the category of 'leopards', the memory task suddenly becomes simple. Consequently, humans use a variety of strategies to judge the importance of information and to integrate it into the ultimate experiences. This process is known as categorization. For easy comprehension, let us consider the following conversation.

It was five o'clock in the evening at Maasai Mara National Reserve, Kenya, in the cold month of August - See Appendix 3. *Punda Milia* the zebra has just been shown round an apartment, which is being offered to let by *Chui* the leopard - proprietor.

Punda Milia: I love it. Can I pay forthwith? Am I the first one to see it?
Chui: ...Yes, you are actually. But there are several others coming round, you know.
Punda Milia: Okay. Then, what is your criterion for selecting the eventual tenant?
Chui: Well, I am going to see the candidates who come along. Then, let them know my decision later.

A while later, a second potential tenant, *Duma* the cheetah, arrives. After being shown round, he asks how the property owner will decide on who will be the tenant.

Duma: Is it on a first come first served... that is, if I wanted it...?

Chui: [*Hesitating*] …yeah …well …yes …someone somewhat suitable I would say yes. But …otherwise, I'll let you know [*embarrassed and awkward laugh*].
Duma: Okay. I like it. But, I have…
Chui: …other options?
Duma: Yes. But, do I have any competition for this one?
Chui: Well… There was a dude who came earlier and …um …but he is Black-striped. Smart looking fellow… But, I thought he might create problems…
Duma: Would you not have a Black-striped…?
Chui: Oh no! I have no problem with the Black-striped. He was a nice herbivore. But, on the other hand, we all know how herbivores behave [*giggles foolishly*]. I thought he might be problematic.
Duma: I do not know what to say. I do not want to lose it; but, I do not want to see my mate treated in a discriminatory way.
Chui: Well, you have to think of yourself first. Look, you are Black-spotted just like me. We are both well cultured. And… we are of a superior breed unlike the Black-striped. We are meat-eaters and cause no trouble.
Duma: Well, I will take it because the Black-striped will not get it anyways?
Chui: You are spot-on. [*He continues his justification for not wanting to let his property to Punda Milia, at one point describing him as uncivilized plant-eater*].

[This is a true story about this author's experience looking for his first apartment in Europe. Nevertheless, similar logic guides all forms of prejudice and negative ethnicity: creation of 'us' versus 'them' dichotomy.]

The above genre of categorization permits ready reference to whole classes of objects without the constant need for particularistic description. When a similar process is applied to humans, it is referred to as social categorization. It is embedded in human cultures and therefore conveyed and reproduced through human interactions.

In almost all the cases, social categorization in humans leads to stereotyping. Further, if it is based on socio-cultural and economic differences between groups, cognitive bias arises. This results in an illusory correlation between the stereotyped group and the frequently occurring attributes. Thus, stereotype becomes prejudice.

I use an example of a fictitious *Ethnic Group Y* to demonstrate how social categorization becomes stereotyping and eventually prejudice. Through social categorization, members of *Ethnic Group Y* are rightly categorized as human beings that seek happiness in their lives. This grouping is therefore based on a feature that actually defines the group – seeking happiness. Dissimilarly, if the process involves characteristics that are unrelated to the criteria for group membership, then it becomes stereotyping. For instance, the *Ethnic Group Y* categorized above, will now be grouped as philanders who only think of personal gain and rapacious humans with loose morals. With these new and unjustifiable characteristics added into the description of *Ethnic Group Y*, stereotype is born. Once it is repeated enough times and eventually held as a 'true' description of the group, the insipid tree of prejudice is ready for fruition. This happens as human beings often notice only those characteristics that are congruent with their stereotypes about 'others'.

From prejudice to negative ethnicity

Prejudice involves negative sentiments directed towards a particular group of people. Viewing prejudice this way is essential as it emphasizes its social consequences for those on the receiving end. Further, it underlines the fact that the perpetrators have engaged in a certain kind of cognitive activity before forming their prejudiced judgement or performing a discriminatory deed.

Leading from the above therefore, when *Chui* in our earlier story makes a 'racist' remark of the type *...but he is Black-striped. I thought he might create problems...* Or, when he chooses to rent his apartment to *Duma* because they are *both Black-spotted and thus of a superior breed unlike the Black-striped Punda Milia*, he has mentally invoked multiple social categories. He uses that categorization as the starting point to infer some negative attributes about *Punda Milia* and to justify his discriminatory actions towards him. This proves that, categorization process is central to the operation of stereotyping without which prejudice would not exist.

Human beings often perceive the world selectively. They use selective perception, as they do not recall incongruent characteristics retrospectively and therefore use the content of stereotypes as the basis for illusory correlations. Thus, they attend to information that supports their stereotypes and ignore information that contradicts them. This process of selective perception gives birth to discrimination as the prejudiced individuals act on their attitudes by victimizing the targeted group. The need to adhere to social norms reinforces the discrimination process as conformity is rewarded and deviations punished. Eventually, this process begets negative ethnicity.

Negative ethnicity has nothing to do with self-pride. It is spiced-up with suspicion and sadistic pleasure in witnessing raw violence. It is a war minus gunshots. For, there is potent toxicity inherent in it that drives reactionary backlash against those of different ethnic backgrounds. It is an elegant disguise for hatred. An alphabet soup of vices: arrogance, bigotry, callousness, deceit, egotism, falseness, greed, hypocrisy, intolerance, jealousy, know-it-all, licentiousness, mediocrity, narcissism, oppression, pomposity, quarrelsomeness, rapacity, selfishness, tyranny, unkindness, vanity, wastefulness, and zealotry.

Flowing from the above therefore, ethnic chauvinism is an idiotic heresy: it fears those it should love and dishonours those it worships. It allows the chauvinists to hide from themselves for it is cold fire that gives no warmth. It misleads, distorts and blinds. It corrodes societal values making its members confuse true with false; good with bad; and, beautiful with ugly. For:

> *Ethnic chauvinism is grisly.*
> *It makes me ugly; and,*
> *Makes you fugly.*
> *It renders us ghastly; and,*
> *Renders Africa unlovely!*

These are facts that should be learnt, and not just learnt, but learnt by heart. Subsequently, one is tempted to ask, do ethnic chauvinists know the difference between the good and the bad? Oh, yes! In fact, I have come across some of them who talk about harmonious co-existence a great deal of the time, and they seem to want peace. But, as soon as they meet their followers in private, they quickly mutate into *Blood-sucking Urchins* – see Chapter 1. Brief, they are like wild animals that come close to you, hoping to get some food, yet run for cover the moment you move toward them in readiness to offer them food. Consequently, they live in an illusionary world based on blatant falsehood, propagated as the complete truth.

Ethnic chauvinists rise on the shoulders of others and need to retain them in that low position. They cannot tolerate that others move from under to join upper ranks, as such a move will make them fall. Thus, they nurture toxic (social-political) environments that make it difficult for others to succeed through merit. They disseminate negative energy to the entire society, which creates selfish followers who follow in order to continue enjoying the stability the status quo offers. Of course, some follow as they are inherently selfish themselves and therefore by default they see those leading chauvinists as absolute models.

Ethnic chauvinists denigrate certain communities, and then do nothing when their followers act on their hatred-infested words and deeds. This is a double-tragedy because, as they rally their supporters, they educate them to hate others while at the same time harnessing existing prejudices. Failure to rein on their lieutenants makes haters feel emboldened and protected.

Ethnic diversity: a source of pride

To confront negative ethnicity, Africans need to expand themselves through knowledge. They need to create a more-inclusive social circle around themselves; and, deliberately strive to positively influence the prejudiced section of the larger society. Because life devoid of ill feelings is a wonderful gift. Towards this end, people need to appreciate the fact that diversity is the essence of humanity. It is an accident of birth and thus it should never be the source of hatred or conflict. For the greater the diversity, the greater the perfection.

That being said, Africa's ethnic diversity should be the source of continental pride. Thus, debates about Africa's identity should not be on how to be homogenous or how to agree on everything. It should be about ensuring that every African has a voice and owns a part of the shared story. For, when Africans tell their story together, they are most truly Africans and most genuinely themselves. Consequently, Africans should be their divine selves, boldly, passionately and respectfully to the absolute best of their ability.

There is strength in the differences between people; as those who are different from you do not impoverish you - they enrich you. For, strength lies in differences, not in similarities. Contrastingly, when one thinks that his path is the only true path, he chains himself to judging others, which narrows his vision of reality. He starts to confuse righteousness with arrogance despite the fact that the path to the former is paved with love while the way to the latter is marked by egotism.

Africans need to develop a sense of oneness in diversity. From that oneness, a spirit of patriotism and African goodwill thrives and binds Africans together as a unified continent. Ultimately, Africa succeeds because of diversity and not in spite of it.

It is never too late to give up your prejudices. Let your life be your message to the world. Make it inspiring to whomever you interact with. Replace 'I' with 'we' any time you think and/or act. And, you will realize even *i*llness becomes *we*llness. This brings us to a story based on my bizarre imagination of a *Far-Far-Away Kingdom*.

One day, a well-known ethnic chauvinist and a devoted evangelical pastor arrived together at *the Kingdom's* gate. After dealing with the necessary formalities, the gatekeeper named Saint Peter took them to their living quarters. First, he led them to a small, single room with a bed, a chair, and a table and announced this was for the clergyman. The chauvinist was worried about what might be in store for him. He could not believe it when Saint Peter stopped in front of a beautiful mansion with lovely grounds, many servants, and told him that these would be his quarters.

Totally lost, the ethnic chauvinist asked the gatekeeper: *how do I get a mansion while that holy man only gets a single room?* Saint Peter answered: *we have thousands and thousands of clergymen/good people while you are the first chauvinist who has ever made it here. In spite of obvious hesitations, you managed to replace 'I' with 'we' in all your acts. That is what we are celebrating today.*

The idea here is simple: with dedication and goodwill, even the most narcissistic ethnic chauvinists can become men of honour. If this is not the case then, my conclusion would be that Saint Peter and his Supervisor weigh the sins of the cold-blooded and those of the warm-hearted on different scales.

Nonetheless, I reiterate that Africa's diversity is not a challenge to overcome. Rather, it is a tremendous source of strength. One of the fundamental elements of humanity and a wellspring of the shared sense of purpose that all Africans should deeply feel. A feeling that irrespective of differing ethnic backgrounds, Africans are united not only in their struggles, but also in their dreams. For they are banded together by an intricate web of mutuality and an inescapable garment of destiny. Individual loyalties must therefore, transcend ethnic groupings and county boundaries. Once this is achieved, diversity becomes a strength. And, Africa's spirit simultaneously grows and glows.

Expanded social contacts as the way forward

Deliberate social contacts between ethnic blocks should be used to reduce negative ethnicity. For this to work, such contacts should take place under three optimal conditions:

(i) Existence of institutional support for the measures designed to promote the social contact;
(ii) Development of meaningful relationships between members of the groups concerned. This can be ensured by contacts that are more frequent and longer in duration; and,
(iii) Identification of co-operative activity that is beneficial to all participants.

Desegregation of the school system at national-level can be the starting point for these social contacts. Intervention programmes based on co-operative learning groups, can further be used to boost intra-group and inter-group interactions. Done well, such desegregation will leave negative ethnicity on the ash-heap of history as it decimates anything that stifles the self-will of the people. Of importance however, the goal should be to dismantle prejudice whilst permitting groups to retain their distinctive identities.

A deeper level of ethnic awareness and appreciation originates from understanding the rationale posited by those who live according to a unique lifestyle. This gradual process requires patience and perseverance. For it takes time to walk in another's shoes; to study other value systems; and, to eventually take relativity seriously.

Once the participants expand their perspectives beyond the immediate; and, see that their views are not the standards by which to measure those of others, African communities and indeed the entire continent will reap immeasurable positive results. In line with this hope therefore, I dream of Africa of diversity.

Africa of diverse dreams

I dream of Africa of di'ersity.
A land devoid of ethnic bigotry.
A continent that's secure in itself.

I dream of Africa of di'erse dreams.
A land confident of its place in the globe.
A continent that's an exemplar of fairness 'n justice;
Tolerance 'n freedom.
A combination that dissolves the dark clouds of negative ethnicity.

Concluding remarks

Cross-ethnic respect is attained when individuals truly believe that the underlying presuppositions of cultural patterns that differ from their own have a validity equal to those beliefs, which support their own way of life. Thus, it is accurate to argue that, cultural understanding furnishes the base for appreciation of ethnic diversity. They understand therefore, that individuals whose cultural patterns vary from their own, value their ethnicity just as much as anyone else does.

Nonetheless, as shown by *Duma*'s reaction to outright prejudice in the first story in this Chapter, those who are not subject to negative ethnicity can sometimes have blind spots or lack appreciation of what it feels like to be on the receiving end. For, one can never really understand another person until he considers things from that person's viewpoint. As we move forward on this journey therefore, let us embrace national policies based on *equal opportunities as an antidote to social exclusion*.

CHAPTER 3

Equal Opportunities: Antidote to Social Exclusion

Exclusivity tears Africa apart

With all human frailties,
Africa remains great.
Still, she can be better,
Fairer 'n more equal;
Through inclusi'ity!

Con'ersely, exclusi'ity tears Africa apart.
It begets deepen'd discontent,
And sharpen'd partisan conflicts.

Exclusi'ity emboldens bigotry;
As politics of falsehood take centre stage.
It turns arguments into animosity;
As disagreement escalates into dehumanization.
For, we judge 'others' by their worst examples;
While we judge 'ourselves' by our best intentions.

Preamble

Equality of opportunity should start with resource allocation and end with the expected outcomes. This ensures that resources are distributed in a manner that equalises outcomes among those exerting the same degree of effort. Consequently, under an equal opportunity set-up, individuals who try equally hard should end up with (almost) similar outcomes.

Consequently, no one should be worse off than others because of circumstances beyond his control. If one does badly through no fault of his own, he should be compensated in some way; but if he fails due to lack of effort, then he should be left to learn his life lesson.

The principle of equal opportunity espoused in this book therefore, is to give everyone what is his due and to demand the contribution of each on the basis of equal consideration. If well implemented, such a policy can go a long way towards tearing down the omnipresent negative ethnicity-based walls in *the Fortress in a Seemingly Peaceful Realm* – see Chapter 2.

Equality in all spheres of life

I learned from my parents at an early age that all rights to be deserved and preserved come from a duty well done. Thus, the very right to live accrues to us only when we diligently perform the duty of citizenship of humanity. Flowing from this quintessential statement therefore, it is easy to define one's duties and correlate every right to some corresponding duty to be performed. That said, any other right that contradicts the foregoing is an usurpation unworthy fighting for.

Later on, my twenty-plus years conducting social science studies brought me in communion with the unique challenges the less privileged face. It opened my heart to the discrimination, both subtle and overt, that they encounter throughout their solemn lives. This was the seed of my unconcealed and oftentimes pointed fight for equal opportunities to all. This genre of equality calls for dismantling of both real and perceived obstacles.

To elucidate this statement, let us re-consider the situation in *the Fortress in a Seemingly Peaceful Realm*. Reformers bring about a change: from now on, membership to *the War Council* will not be drawn exclusively from the wealthy stratum of *the Fortress*. Members will instead be selected on the basis of a competitive examination in military prowess. The entry exam will be open to anyone willing to join this elite group.

However, it turns out that only scions of the wealthy stratum pass the exam and join *the War Council*. How so? Everyone in *the Fortress* except the wealthy is poorly nourished, and being well nourished is a prerequisite for developing skills needed to succeed on the competitive entry-level examination.

In this setting therefore, the reformers only replaced the old explicit obstacle with an implicit one. As a result, *the War Council* continues to be dominated by the wealthy in the society, for the poor will never satisfy the eligibility requirements for admission. This is so because, inequality shuts the gates of opportunity and propagates the cycle of poverty with all its derivatives.

> **WAR COUNCIL INTERVIEW DIRECTIVE**
> For fairness-sake and in the spirit of equal opportunities, all candidates must do the same test.

I use a real example to validate the foregoing. My first charity-oriented activity was teaching traditional martial arts to homeless/street children aged between eight and seventeen years in Eldoret town, Kenya – see Appendix 3. Often my students came to training hungry – no breakfast, no lunch and no dinner. Therefore, the two-hour sessions twice a week started with a light snack then ended with sharing of some food. Every day, I wished there was more that I could do. Nevertheless, I remained determined to equip my young trainees with the tested coping strategies inherent in traditional martial arts – fairness, justice, respect, discipline, perseverance, humility among others -, hoping that they will come in handy in the future.

My students did not know why others disliked them. However, they knew the pain of prejudice and inequality, because it was evident in their innocent eyes. Seeing the scars of poverty and hatred on hopeful faces of young children is a heart-wrenching experience. It entirely changed the way I look at life. Today, however, I am elated by your acceptance to join me on this sacred journey of helping the sons and daughters of those students and people like them across Africa. You did this by purchasing a copy of this book as all proceeds go to charity in aid of the less privileged children.

In the example just sketched, my students cum homeless children would have no opportunity to serve *the Fortress in a Seemingly Peaceful Realm* through *the War Council* even with the re-formulated selection criteria. For, it is absolute dishonesty to say that a poor child attending an under-resourced (public) school has the same opportunities of advancement as a rich child attending an ultra-resourced (private) school. This should be a common sense-driven view. Consequently, I challenge you dear reader to play your part, at any point and in whatever capacity, to ensure that all members of society have the opportunity to sharpen their skills.

One can therefore, imagine *the Fortress in a Seemingly Peaceful Realm* taking a variety of steps to provide opportunities to all. Availing nutrition supplements to those with inadequate diet. Offering scholarships to the underprivileged. Dispatching extra teachers to every village to help those interested in acquiring proficiency at set skills. Once this is done and the final selection process remains objective, then equality opens the city of hope to all. Only then, will my students and their generations back in Eldoret have the opportunity to enter *the War Council* in the service of *the Fortress*.

The equality of opportunity ideals canvassed to this point have been designed mainly for application to the economic sphere of life broadly construed. When opportunities are equal, people have equal chances to get ahead. However, it is not obviously the case that when people advance equal opportunity claims, the background ideal to which they are appealing is limited to any one sphere of social life. Historic struggles throughout the world have been waged to secure equal voting rights and equal rights to participate in the political process for disenfranchised groups including women, those disfavoured on racial grounds and sexual orientations, and members of lower-ranked social-castes. The vote can be used to advance one's economic interests but its significance is not limited to that. Having the freedom to participate in political affairs on the same terms as other members of society is an element in being a full member of society equal in fundamental status to all others.

Democratic equality is akin to equal opportunity in the sphere of politics. This justifies the need to limit the impact of wealthy political donors on the democratic political process in Africa. Thus, countries in the continent should institute public funding of political parties and restrictions on private donations to political campaigns in order to make progress toward approximating the democratic equality ideal.

When wide formal equality of opportunity is satisfied in a society, people also receive equal treatment in the judicial system. Thus, one's likelihood of success in legal proceedings depends only on the merits of his case. The same holds for other public services and non-competitive services from private firms and not-for-profit agencies. For example, if you are in medical need, and have purchased a specific type of medical insurance coverage, you receive similar quality of service like all other subscribers. In other words, you do not receive better or worse care depending on how the service provider is disposed to respond to your salient group membership. Similar standard is held when you are a customer in a restaurant, a client of a professional golf trainer, an applicant for a driver's license among others.

If this universal freedom from prejudice and distrust is common knowledge among members of society, one might plausibly conjecture that such knowledge becomes a basis of social solidarity and general civility. Ultimately, it smoothens the relationships between ethnic blocks, which hugely reduces negative ethnicity as detailed elsewhere in this book.

Government and equal opportunities

The government of the day appoints hundreds of citizens to serve in varying capacities. These appointees make decisions about myriad aspects of the people's socio-cultural and economic lives. Thus, such appointments should reflect respective country's cultural mosaic. For this to happen, the appointment processes must be transparent, accessible and equitable for all.

Thus, government jobs should go to the most qualified. Similarly, economic opportunities should be seized by anyone irrespective of whether or not one's parents are of 'noble blood' or cronies of the ruling elite. This would work only when jobs on offer are publicized both openly and in advance, so that anyone interested has a reasonable opportunity to apply. In this setting formal equality of opportunity also requires that:

- ❖ All applications that meet minimum requirements are accepted;
- ❖ They are judged on their merits; and,
- ❖ The most qualified according to the laid down criteria are offered positions.

Granting opportunities based on personal connections rather than standardised merit undercuts the principals of transparency that should be central to the hiring and contracting processes. This leads to the provision of inferior services and products, which, weakens employees' morale as well as public faith in the integrity of government – see Chapter 2. Once this becomes the standard of operation, a seed of discord is sewn. With time, it sprouts and develops into a full-blown tree of intra- and interethnic group conflicts. Finally, it bears fruits in the form of ethnic chauvinism well marked by ferocious *Blood-sucking Urchins.*

As discussed in the previous chapter, national/continental cohesion borne-out diversity has enormous potential. To harness it however, the public sector must be grounded on sound ethical values. Values driven by unwavering commitment to the rule of law and equality of opportunity to all regardless of ethnic backgrounds. Further, Africans should always entertain contrasting point of views. For divergence in opinions generates creative tensions that fuel innovation and strategic foresight, which is essential for a vibrant community.

Moreover, any African community is diverse with equally varying abilities. By working together - having the old mentor the young; the young inspiring the old; and the strong helping the weak -, Africans give fully. For, when united a people's power is illimitable and as a continent, Africa shall have succeeded when a child born into the depressing poverty knows that he has the same opportunity to succeed as anybody else. When he knows he is important and equal. Leading from the above thence, I hope for a future where hatred against some groups of people will not be the operative rule in any society within *the Fortress in a once Seemingly Peaceful Realm.*

I hope for a moment when every single African realizes that it does not matter if one is a 'rose' or a 'water-lilly' or a 'bristle-grass'. What matters is that he is flowering. And, as he flowers, he keeps in mind that his ethnic background is just one model of reality. The remaining ethnic groupings are not in any way failed attempts at being him. Rather, they are unique manifestations of the very human spirit. The human beauty that makes Africa unique.

Concluding remarks

Africa's concern for equal opportunity for all should be firm and unshakable. The continent should adopt it as her new norm in order to dismantle the omnipresent crippling legacy of favouritism. Once done, it will brighten the lives of all as liberty requires opportunity to make a living that is decent according to the standard of the time. A level of standard that gives one not only enough to live by, but something to live for. This is essential when dealing with ethnic-related divisions.

Beyond this book is the outraged conscience of a continent and the harsh judgment of history on actions and/or inactions by all Africans. Thus, no one should be denied the possibility to participate in national building. For equality bestows dignity to humanity as it is insensitive to one's possessions and appearance. It rests on his right to be treated as equal among others and enables him to live in accordance to his ability and merits. Once the *Fortress in a once Seemingly Peaceful Realm* realizes the foregoing, Africans will together in the spirit of African brotherhood, walk out of the *deep dark tunnels of economic, social and political corruption.*

CHAPTER 4

Economic, Social and Political Corruption

Deep dark tunnels of corruption

Proud 'n loud.
We teach our children wrong from wrong.
How to screw others for personal gain.
How to taste another hive's honey by violatin' the queen bee.
How to satisfy self as others die.
In the name of corruption.

We close our eyes.
Lest we see things we hate to admit.
Surpris'd by non-existing surprises;
All colourful pills become sweet tastin' skittles.
In our clogg'd minds, righteousness lacks.
In our crook'd hearts, deep dark tunnels of graft reign.
Darkenin' the virtue of the land.
For, air, light 'n water;
Go to the highest bidder.
At the command of corruption goddess.

Not all is lost;
For, you're an instrument.
Play your life story;
Sing your mind; and,
Bleed your words.
Anti-corruption words.

Preamble

Corruption exists in developed and developing countries; in public and private sectors; and, in not-for-profit and charitable organizations. Even religious entities are not safe in *the Fortress in a once Seemingly Peaceful Realm* as illustrated in the following factual dialogue between a rich worshiper and his 'wicked' pastor.

> *Worshiper:* I would like you to say a Mass for my dead pet dog.
> *Pastor:* [*Indignantly*] What do you mean, say a Mass for your dog?
> *Worshiper:* I really loved that pet and I would like you to offer a Mass for him.
> *Pastor:* We do not offer Masses for dogs here. I suggest you try other religious groups down the street.
> *Worshiper:* [*Leaving the Parish Office, he murmured*] Too bad. I really loved that pet. I was planning to offer a million-dollar stipend for the Mass in his honour.
> *Pastor:* [*Enlivened*] Wait a minute, you never told me your pet worshiped God...

[...And, the crooked 'holy' pastor got the stipend!]

It is worth noting that although this chapter examines economic, social and political corruption separately, the demarcation line is not always evident. This is only done to boost the fluidity of the discourse that ensues.

Corruption muddles life itself

Corruption occurs when business operations infringe on set rules. Observance of rules is essential to counter dark-dealings. Such an observation:

- ❖ Maintains a sense of fair play;
- ❖ Prevents conflicts of interest;

- ❖ Checks greed and other uncivilized human instincts; and,
- ❖ Minimizes socially undesirable consequences.

Generally, respect of the set rules ensures that economic undertakings proceed in an orderly and predictable fashion.

When benefits are large; chances of being caught are small; and, penalties when caught are light; then many people will embrace corruption. Individuals will have no incentive to try to change it or to refrain from taking part in it. Once it becomes systemic and the majority of people operate under it, a maze of interlocking jurisdictions and multiple layers of government confronts average citizens in trying to solve even the simplest of problems. This aptly captures my experience after the murder of my brother Hillary.

That dreadful Saturday afternoon, my sister called me and amidst sobs told me: *Hillary's heavily tortured body is lying at City Mortuary in Nairobi* - see Appendix 3. I was shocked. This cannot be true, I thought to myself. Eventually, I read my *Life Lesson: For the love of humanity, have no moral middle ground and refuse indifference as an option to violence. Be unyielding and inflexible in its opposition. Make a difference.*

Over the next several weeks, I was told in excruciatingly vivid details about the events that led up-to Hillary's death. I learnt that my brother had a professional-related disagreement with his employer, a scion of a wealthy and political dynasty in Kenya – See Appendix 2. [My brother had detailed this disagreement to me a week before he was murdered.] In a pre-arranged manner, one of his colleagues invited him for an evening drink. At about midnight, he was tricked out of the building along Moi Avenue, downtown Nairobi, and two undercover police officers forced him into a waiting car. The following morning, the police 'collected' his mutilated body at the edge of Karura Forest within Nairobi City. According to the private post-mortem, my brother was heavily tortured. He was hit with a blunt object, read gun-butt, on the back of his head several times causing multiple fractures on the skull. Then, he was strangulated. As in many other similar cases in this part of the world, Hillary was labelled a dangerous armed criminal.

With the risk of re-living this ordeal, I feel obliged to state that: coming from a humble beginning, we were taught from an early age the importance of hard and honest work. No short cuts. No, Hillary would never be involved in any uncalled-for activity. He was not a criminal. He was a respected aeronautical engineering instructor at an aviation college in Nairobi.

After Hillary's burial, I promised my aging mother that I would do whatever it takes for justice to be done. I badly wanted to know what happened to my brother. Unearthing the specific details that lead to his killing was like peeling an onion. The outer skin came out with some difficulties, but in no time, I was in its innards, which caused tears to stream freely from my eyes, and my heart. It was like ripping open an old wound every second, every minute, every hour, and every day for months. The pain was, and remains, both palpable and excruciating.

Paradoxically, rather than offering answers, the information provided by the law enforcers raised more questions. Questions that remain unanswered for my family. The casual manner in which the police officers treated our enquiries left us totally devastated. I could not understand how an officer who has taken a solemn oath to protect lives would in a condescending fashion advice a distraught family to: *shallow the pride; take the fucking body; bury it; and, forget about the bastard.* Hillary's body was not a fucking body and he was not a bastard!

Despite the pain all this caused me; it triggered the desire to shed-light on police brutality and official corruption, which impede justice in *the Fortress in a once Seemingly Peaceful Realm*. But, as time went by, things changed! Streets, houses, urban centres and people appeared different depending on the state of my mind. Nairobi, for instance, looked sullen and hostile. The presence of police officers tore my fragile soul while some crowds among whom I enjoyed company filled me with dismay. Everything felt so alien, hostile, and utterly meaningless. My life took a real beating.

Two consecutive senior investigative officers were transferred to far-flung stations once they had connected the crucial dots related to my brother's killing. The third officer was openly fearful the moment he was assigned my brother's murder file. He became very uncooperative. The endless death threats that I received through emails, telephone calls and text messages worsened my nightmares. Those pursuing me obtained my new cellular phone number as soon as I changed it. They stopped me almost anywhere at any time; and, warned me of dire consequences if I continued with the investigation on my brother's killing. The more I maintained my resolve on the matter, the more they upped their threats. A squad of goons would enter my residential compound at the wee hours of the night; wake me up by sadistically knocking on my bedroom window. Then, in a coordinated fashion, they would flash their short hand-guns. They would send text messages after their uncalled for visits warning me: *we are only waiting for the final signal to kill you*. I lived every day under the threat of death. I had innumerable frustrating and bewildering nights.

I religiously reported these threats to the local police station. Each time, the police officers on duty would crudely advise me to decide whether I want to live or to join my brother in hell. I would respond: *I do not need to join Hillary in hell. For I am living in hell in my own country*. This response once infuriated an *Officer Commanding Police Division* (OCPD) in one of the police stations in Nairobi. He roughed me while in his office and threatened to lock me in. The presence of my lawyer, Doug, could not dent his determination to teach me a lesson. My lawyer was kidnapped on his way back to Eldoret town, a few days later. His badly tortured body was 'discovered' about ten kilometres from Nakuru town while his car, which he was driving was abandoned in a different part of the said urban centre – see

Appendix 3. Thereafter, I lived in a state of uninterrupted deep anxiety interspersed with spells of suicidal depression. No one noticed! Today, it feels as if I am describing somebody else's life. [I spare the rest of the story for another day].

Nonetheless, this experience taught me that when we meet tragedy in life, we can react in two ways: either lose hope and fall into self-destructive habits; or, use the challenge to find our inner-strength. Therefore, the twin barbarous killings inspired me to serve fellow beings by not focusing my energy on fighting the old, but on building the new. For, change itself is painless, only the resistance to it is painful. Subsequently, I decided to:

> *Change the changeable.*
> *Ne'er allow the unchangeable to dim my happiness;*
> *And, remo'e myself from the unacceptable.*
> *For, fightin' against the future's an act in futility.*

In sum, faced with endless deep dark tunnels of corruption, I did not know where to turn for answers; who to hold accountable; who to praise; and, who to blame. A predicament many Africans live with in their daily lives. That said, a less serious story is timely:

Mr. Swara the antelope was running hither and thither in search of safety outside his home in the oftentimes frigid Mount Kenya National Park, Kenya – See Appendix 3. He met his girlfriend *Ms. Twiga* the giraffe, and a conversation arose…
    Ms. Twiga: [*Concerned*] Why are you running dear?
    Mr. Swara: [*Outwardly startled*] Police officers are
              indiscriminately arresting all goats.
    Ms. Twiga: But, you aren't a goat!
    Mr. Swara: It will take you the rest of your life to prove that
              in the courts in *the Fortress in a once Seemingly*
              Peaceful Realm.
[…And, *Ms. Twiga* started running!]

Economic corruption: the sand in the wheels

From an economic standpoint, three primary areas attract high-level corruption in Africa. They are government contracts, government taxes and regulatory processes. Firstly, corrupt deals influence the outcome and terms of government tenders and contracts. This includes importation of goods that are on high demand but in short supply. Further, issuance of licenses and permits for lucrative economic projects are based on who is capable and willing to partake in underground payments.

Secondly, government taxes serve as a lucrative avenue for corruption. Through dark dealings, individuals and business firms reduce the amount of taxes, fees, custom duties, and other public utility charges that they pay for government services and products.

Thirdly, weak regulatory processes attract many corrupt players. They offer bribes to quicken the processes. In other cases, the regulatory authorities are enticed to refrain from taking the necessary punitive measures when the concerned party contravenes set procedures, rules, regulations and/or laws.

Some would argue that economic corruption is necessary for growth as it 'greases the wheels' of development. In reality, corruption is 'the sand in the wheels' that impedes growth as it contributes to many pernicious effects on efficiency. To start with, corruption binds Africans in an imperial cage and blinds them to their humanistic potential - the potential to realize a thriving society for all. A society where people share and understand each other, instead of a society where division and pain are valued as a source of power.

Like unequal opportunity, discussed in Chapter 3, corruption lowers the quality of Africa's public infrastructure and services. It depletes the tax base and distorts government expenditure. Fraud, embezzlement and misappropriation of public funds exacerbate the losses. This leaves little money for public workers' salaries and provision of infrastructure and superstructures as the government is caught up in a recurring shortage of operation and development funds. Subsequently, it results in over-borrowing in an attempt to remedy the crippling bottlenecks in the national economy or to ease the hardships that the ordinary people face in their daily lives.

Corruption generates economic rents and rent seeking. Thus, actors secure above-normal returns from an asset not by adding value to it through investment, but rather, through manipulating socio-economic and political environments. As used in this book therefore, rent-seeking activities include bribery, fraud, graft, and all other shady deals that involve misuse of public office. Hence, economic rent benefits only a small section of the population in *the Fortress in a once Seemingly Peaceful Realm* resulting in uneven income distribution.

Corruption adversely affects national's domestic and foreign investments. For entrepreneurs have to bribe their way through the inception stage to the operational phases of their business operations. Consequently, in many cases, they engage dubious agents who have mastered how to get around through the maze of the nerve-racking corrupt rules. Thus, corruption raises the initial costs of investment and increases the level of uncertainty for an economic venture. It becomes a regressive form of tax, which results in depletion of government revenue. If unabated, tax evasion could equal any given country's national budget. Ironically, the tax evaders' economic crimes in Africa are camouflaged behind the masks of large bungalows, expensive possessions, big cars and inexhaustible bank balances.

Social rules and corruption

In all African countries, like elsewhere in the world, there are a myriad of rules and regulations that are meant to serve social objectives and to ensure public safety. They include building codes, environmental controls and traffic laws. Violation of such rules for personal gain leads to social disruptions. Unfortunately, such occurrences are common in *the Fortress in a once Seemingly Peaceful Realm.*

Non-observance of building codes by contractors who connive with corrupt officials has resulted in the collapse of many buildings across Africa. In many cases, contractors use short cuts and substandard building materials to boost their profits.

Use of substandard materials and non-adherence to engineering specifications form another corruption-related menace. Combined they have resulted in bridges collapsing and dams bursting, which lead to loss of life and property.

Road accidents claim hundreds of lives daily. Many reasons are given to explain this phenomenon: un-roadworthy and poorly maintained vehicles; reckless driving; and, corrupt traffic police officers. Additionally, roads continue to be designed and built without sufficient attention to the needs of the most vulnerable road users.

Financial malpractice is a common feature in Africa's banking sector. This is a result of compromised supervision of monetary systems, which causes far-reaching negative socio-economic consequences. For instance, many people have lost their savings due to the collapse of unaccountable banking institutions.

Political corruption

Corruption corrodes political processes. It opens the door to tension and frustration, which undermines democracy and genuine social change. It exacerbates divisions and sufferings thereby solidifying the concealed socio-economic and political caste system in *the Fortress in a once Seemingly Peaceful Realm*. This transforms public processes into a cacophony of folly in which Africans fight among themselves as they try to outdo one another. They waste their energy and resources in maintaining and strengthening the cycle of corruption. Eventually, national politics become a game of musical chairs whose intensity is determined by national elections.

The high costs of elections motivate political parties to prefer self-financing candidates who contribute economic rent to their coffers. At the same time, the unregulated political party financing system leads to parties and candidates under-reporting their collections and expenses. Thus, political party financing is one of the clearest avenue for grand (political) corruption in many African countries.

Domination of party politics by a few super-rich personalities and lack of inner-party democracy promote corruption. This is compounded by the fact that politicians throughout the continent dispense favours to their political allies in order to win or sustain cooperation and loyalty. Subsequently, a form of politics that revolves around the creation of personalities is born. This is followed by a rapid increase of a breed of people who yearn for admission into the corridors of power at any cost.

There is an informal expectation for the elected officials throughout Africa to make financial contributions to diverse social welfare-related projects to the benefit of their constituents. Such projects include but are not limited to: weddings; birthday parties; marriage-related ceremonies; and, a wide spectrum of traditional festivities. This is an added financial burden to the officials, which motivates them to engage in rent seeking as described elsewhere in this Chapter. It is clear therefore, that there are undeniable socio-cultural, economic and political imperatives that entice elected leaders in Africa into underground dealings.

Corruption falls heavily on the poor

When corruption becomes a way of life, peoples' behaviour and attitudes, institutions and rules are attuned to the corruption *modus operandi*. In this state of affair, the burden of corruption falls heavily on those who cannot afford to pay the required bribes for various types of services and products. In almost all the cases, these happen to be the hard working poor members of the society. Therefore, it is safe to argue that corruption takes necessities from the masses to give luxuries to the classes. It rewards the poor with a mere living and bestows crooks with all magnificence of modern life.

This reminds me of an experience a couple of years ago at the Kenya's Coastal region. From a tourism perspective, this region is the ideal area to experience the real tropical beach tourism. It is a well-established resort area – but that is just an anecdote to the current discussion. Of relevance is the operation of a certain multi-million dollar golf course located a couple of kilometres from Mombasa City - See Appendix 3. Through clandestine connections to the main water supply, the watering system in the golf course operates twenty-four hours a day, seven days a week, twelve months a year, to keep the grass fresh and green. At the same time, the local residents in the neighbourhood use unsafe water for their household needs. At night, through a similar arrangement, bribing public officers, the golf course remains lighted throughout the night, while local children in the neighbouring dilapidated residential estates do their school homework by candlelight.

Courtesy of the community-based tourism project that I was managing in the region, I met with the materially rich owner of the said golf course. He told me:

> I give back to the community in a big way. I have dug boreholes for many families. I spend thousands of dollars on academic scholarships for the top-two performers in the nearby elementary schools. I love my people. I truly care for them. They would hardly survive without me. In fact, without my investment in the golf course, this entire region would have remained underdeveloped.

Do you see the anomaly inherent in this twisted argument? That is not charity! It is self-interest masquerading under the form of altruism. The golf course owner is only contributing towards personal rewards, to erase sins, to assuage bad conscience and to make impressions. For he takes away from the poor people with the left-hand; then, gives back some with his right-hand. Worse than Robin Hood – the one of 'robbing from the rich and giving to the poor' saga. For, he is only driven by the likely consequences, with economic advantage as his goal.

Let me complicate this even more. At times, I have this mysterious imagination of a King in the fictional *Far-Far-Away Kingdom* (the one alluded to in Chapter 2) saying to his subjects: *I was hungry and you gave me something to eat. I was thirsty and you gave me something to drink. I was a stranger and you invited me in.* And, the people seated at the front row joyously shoot back: *Alleluia! That is correct, Lord. We know!* Dispirited, the King responds: *I was not talking to you, idiots! It does not follow the script; you are not supposed to have known.*

The thrust of this argument is simple: true charity is when you do something good without the notion that you are doing anything good. For,

> *A good's ne'er so good;*
> *As when you're unaware that you're doin' good.*
> *You're ne'er so good;*
> *As when you're unconscious that you're good.*
> *For a saint's one,*
> *Till he knows it!*
> *And, a tiger ne'er proclaims its tigritude.*

Let me make one thing plain: I look at genuine charity as the essence of goodness. It implies love that understands. A kind of love that does not merely share the wealth of the giver, but in true empathy and wisdom helps the receiver to help himself. Nonetheless, corruption has corroded the modern form of charity. It has become like a rose, the most beautiful flower on earth. A flower that has been reduced to a mere element of ritual: it is thrown on the new-borns and the dead; decorated in places of worship and war memorials; splashed on the newly wed and the just divorced; and, given to religious leaders and tyrants.

As I say this, I am fully aware that I risk being castigated by those whose personal designs I put in jeopardy by revealing their shallowness. Nonetheless, I am motivated by the need to establish a perfect slogan for charity, and at the end, I hope, it will become clear that it is not merely masquerading in the garb of an authentic concern. To finalize my thesis therefore, I maintain that genuine charity intends to improve the welfare of the receiver and never to massage the giver's runaway ego.

ACTIONABLE CORRUPTION STRATEGIES

*One generation plants the trees,
Another enjoys the shade.*
(Chinese Proverb)

Realistic corruption strategies must appreciate the fact that there is demand for and supply of corruption. There are those who demand acts of corruption and there are public employees willing to perform these acts at a fee. Largely though, it is the state that creates the environment and the incentives that influence those who pay and those who accept and/or demand bribes through its policies and (lack of) actions.

Thus, anti-corruption enforcement measures in *the Fortress in a once Seemingly Peaceful Realm* cannot be effective in the absence of a serious effort to address the underlying causes: biting poverty, crippling unemployment, widening inequality, and paralysing social exclusivity. In this scenario, Africa is faced with the stubborn socio-economic and political reality whereby the majority of the citizens are trapped on the margins of the society. They are left alone contending with the multiple crises of: unjustifiable landlessness; man-made homelessness; absence of basic services; prevalence of fatal diseases such as HIV/AIDS and malaria; unceasing food insecurity; abundance of (illegal) narcotics; and, unparalleled levels of crime and violence.

As a result, Africa is today highly polarized, in which the fault lines of ethnicity, class and religion run deep – see for example Chapter 2. To worsen this situation, a silo-mentality persists in Africa even after half a century of independence from the devastating yokes of colonialism. Many (political) leaders throughout the continent lack the basic understanding of the role of subsidiarity. This brings forth a pattern of mutual hostility, arrogance and/or indifference, which subverts any cross-ethnic collaboration.

Under such a climate of fragmentation, anti-poverty strategies fail to bring the relevant players together. Consequently, inclusive processes are replaced with quick-fix solutions, which are based on one-size fits all models. In this confusion therefore, initiatives are top-heavy on policy but light on delivery mechanisms. As the first step towards the eradication of any form of corruption, African nations need to replace these top-down approaches with bottom-up policy frameworks, which favour:

- ❖ Efficient utilization of resources;
- ❖ Reduction of bureaucratic red tape;
- ❖ Movement of power to common people; and,
- ❖ Capitalization on the diverse contributions, innovation and civic energy of all stakeholders.

My thesis here is that no single set of actors, can exclusively tackle the challenges of entrenched social exclusion. A more inclusive model premised on broader public accountability, transparency, good governance and cooperation could realise this. Such a model provides an essential rallying point around which dynamic, long-term and value-driven partnerships are forged.

It is worth noting in passing that, no one contributes as much to the survival of the less fortunate in *the Fortress in a once Seemingly Peaceful Realm* as the poor themselves. They do so through a range of self-propelling informal mechanisms such as neighbour-helping-neighbour, savings groups commonly known as *chama*, burial groups among others. They creatively enact social solidarity in a very simple and practical manner. Individually and/or collectively such initiatives play a vital role in giving voice to the poor. They ensure effective mobilisation of resources and collective action, and take forward actionable agendas for pro-poor transformation. These can be the springboards for an anti-corruption crusade by taking the best practices at the local level then amplify them to a national/continental scale.

With this in mind therefore, all levels of governments in Africa should bridge dialogue. They should speak for the weak; hear the broken cries of the poor; and, give voice to the voiceless. Eventually, they would establish a more level playing field in which citizens play a meaningful role in multi-directional and all-inclusive sustainable development. This underscores the need for Africans to ceaselessly recreate themselves.

To realize such a recreation,
E'eryone must have a heart that ne'er hardens;
A temper that ne'er tires;
A touch that ne'er hurts;
And, a heart that ne'er hurts.

Such a heart enables one to realize that to be aware of a single shortcoming in oneself is more useful than to be aware of a thousand in another fellow being. And, by relentlessly reminding another that he is unwise, does not make you any wiser. Once Africans do this, they will perceive corruption-linked challenges anew. They will see them through each other's eyes thereby forging a common purpose despite varied viewpoints. This is called unity in diversity.

Subsequently, the continent will be able to convert the biting poverty into positive energy. This would be the key starting point towards the demolition of the inherent power and resource imbalances, which reinforce poverty and powerlessness throughout *the Fortress in a once Seemingly Peaceful Realm.* Eventually, this results in transformation of all lives through horizontal and vertical exchanges of resources and support within and between communities throughout Africa.

Corruption needs to be pursued from three fronts

Just as there is no 'one size fits all' policy for economic development, there is no such a policy for fighting corruption. The response to corruption needs to be as complex and variegated as corruption itself. Thus, due to its complexity, corruption must be pursued from three major fronts.

First, ensure honest, persistent and visible commitment by the leadership to fight corruption of all forms. When top (political) leaders fail to provide the right example, it cannot be expected that public servants will behave differently.

Second, increase incentives towards honest behaviour on the public servants while at the same time increasing the risks associated with corrupt deals. This should be complemented by a relentless campaign to create awareness on the ill-effects of corruption. Such a crusade should involve citizens of all walks of life.

Third, adhere to meritocracy and fairness in all appointments – see also Chapter 3. On the same strength, oversight bodies should ensure that civil servants are insulated from political interference. Otherwise, the public service will be rendered toothless or even worse, misused for political gain. Further, the anti-corruption bodies must have personnel of unquestionable integrity.

Concluding remarks

Uncontestably, there is no quick fix for economic, social and political corruption. As a people however, Africans must realize that they shall never find the light unless, like a candle, they are willing to be their own fuel. Then, they allow that light to unite them so that they can together unshackle themselves from these debilitating manacles of this degeneracy - *The Blood-sucking Urchins*.

All Africans must create the necessary anti-corruption conditions. For, it is not enough to talk about and pray for zero-corruption. They must believe in it first; then individually and collectively take appropriate actions - walk the talk! For, work is accomplished by doing it, not talking about it. Once all is said and done, there is an urgent need to cut unnecessary procedural hassles that cause delay and hindrances in almost every little bit of good. This will boost the morale of the people. When the morale of a nation rises, looting decreases and the need to take shortcuts for greedy reasons diminishes. This calls Africans to walk and work together, which reminds me of a little bird's story.

One day a monstrous fire broke out at Lake Nakuru National Park, Kenya - See Appendix 3. A huge savannah was suddenly engulfed by a raging wildfire. Frightened, all the resident animals fled out of the park. Bemoaning the destruction of their homes, they all believed there was nothing they could do about the fire, except for *Kolibri* the hummingbird. *Kolibri* swooped into a nearby stream; picked-up drops of water with her microscopic beak; flew back to the burning savannah; and, put the droplets onto the fire. She went back and forth. Other animals watched in disbelief. Some commented: *what a futile effort? You're too tiny. They're only droplets. You can't put out this fire.* Then, their forlorn leader declared: *I have done my part!* His deputy followed suit and asked *Kolibri*: *What the hell do you think you're doing?* Unhesitatingly, she answered: *I am doing my bit.*

Like *Kolibri*, do your little bit of good wherever you are in order to dent the enormity of this egregious fire of corruption engulfing Africa. It is those little tidbits of good put together that will make the continent corrupt-free.

Poverty, unemployment, social exclusion and marginalisation breed resentment. When opportunities are skewed due to favouritism, people lose trust in the system – see Chapter 3. Mistrust kicks in which begets fear. Fear gives birth to hopelessness, which is the most dangerous state of humankind as it creates desperation. Desperation forces citizens to embrace all sorts of shortcuts, which give birth to socio-economic and political corruption. This fuels hatred that ignites violence thereby transforming Africa into *hell on earth as in violence, humanity loses.*

CHAPTER 5

In Violence, Humanity Loses

Hell on earth

Non-violence makes heaven on earth.
Causes external, internal 'n eternal bliss.
Taken at true value.
You're all I want.
You're everythin' I love.
For, you're I.

Violence begets hell on earth.
Causes external 'n internal turmoil.
When taken at face value.
It is nothin' but a bruise.
Not an abuse.
You'll be fine.
For, you're like I.

Violence is hell.
Causes external, internal 'n eternal distress.
When taken for grant'd.
You're a pathetic spell.
You're no longer what I want.
You're everythin' I hate.
For, you're unlike I; and,
You aren't I.
For, in violence, humanity loses!

Preamble

Both men and women have innate potential for being violent. For a man is not violent because of being in a male body. He becomes violent, or otherwise, in the process of exhibiting the hallmarks of normalised masculinity. Subsequently, abuse and violence result from a sense of entitlement, not because it is a male characteristic.

A similar argument holds true for a woman. Thus, the genre of violence discussed in this book is gender insensitive. This is the type of violence experienced within the limits of *the Fortress in a once Seemingly Peaceful Realm*.

Beating of a mentally unstable man

I encountered raw violence at a tender age. That afternoon on my way home from elementary school, I noticed a group of five senior boys from my school surrounding a man with tattered clothes and dirty shoes. I went closer; and, I realized it was Mister Charles Njogu - a mentally unstable man from my boyhood village. Some boys poked him with sticks while others bombarded him with tiny stones. The sudden screaming scared daylights out of him, and fear was written all over his face. He quivered like a limbless man in a lion's den. The more distressed he became, the more his torturers furthered their torturing game. He was frightened. Wherever he turned for safety he was attacked and thrown back to the middle of his ferocious tormentors. He ran in circles with the frenzy of a trapped animal.

As I watched this, tears flowed freely from some inextinguishable source of sadness. It made me both angry and irritated. I walked up to the delinquents, and jumped in the middle next to Charles. From my little height, I looked the ringleader in the eyes, and asked him politely to order his gang to stop their heinous act. I recited to them what my mother, Sephora, had all along taught me: *if you have nothing good to offer this man, offer him nothing. Leave him alone!* In a coordinated manner, they turned their attention to me. All of a sudden, my small size became pronounced and equated to their earlier victim's handicap. Their leader set on me with a succession of stomping kicks battering me to earth. The rest of the devilish team followed suit. They levied blow after blow on my tiny body. I fought back with all my strength but came-out badly beaten. My mouth and nostrils oozed blood; my vision got dark; my senses blurred; my gallbladder momentarily stopped functioning while a deafening ringing emanated from my ears. In the process, Charles managed to run away. That was my main achievement.

At first, the episode was too vague to relate to my mother. I tried to remember the incident, but the whole story jumbled up and disintegrated into incomprehensible pieces that floated uselessly in my eleven-year-old brain. *Is Charles fine? Where did he go? Why did they have to do this to him? What will happen to him?* These were some of the questions that would come and go in rushes with no adequate answers. Disjointed matters shuffled and reshuffled in my tiny head until I was totally blank. Nevertheless, my caring mother washed and treated my wounds.

When the strange view of Charles being beaten-up did not reappear, I regained my composure and narrated to my mother what happened. She lauded me saying:

> I am proud of you son. You were not only a voice for the voiceless, but you rendered a voice to one who has none. You lent him what the 'Almighty' has freely given you. These bruises should forever remind you that there are always painful battles before victory; and, that good things come with the determination to keep trying when the going gets tough - she concluded. [The rest is a story for another day].

Charles' beating was not a mere event; it is a living example. It confirms the extent of commitment required when a man becomes aware of an injustice to another human being. With time and space, methods keep changing, the fire rages differently, but the source remains the same. Motivated by the same injustice. As an eleven-year old boy, I did not understand the significance of my sweet mother's words, but each time I look at the permanent scars that I got from that beating, I see in them the vision of my future, the purpose of my life and the necessity of my mission. I vowed thereafter that one day, I will be able to defend myself and those in need of my defence no matter how long it takes. I do so more efficiently through my writings.

Some fellow humans are excited by raw violence

Lapses in the maintenance of social order lead to loss of official power. This results in chaos, which is the science of surprises. This ushers us into *Chaos Theory* that deals with nonlinear things that are effectively impossible to predict or control, like turbulence, weather, the stock market, human brain states, and so on. Recognizing the chaotic, fractal nature of our world can give us new insight, power, and wisdom to avoid actions which may end up being detrimental to our long-term well-being. Nonetheless, this seems easier said than done in Africa's existent socio-economic and political systems. This conundrum is well captured by the following story that I use in class when elucidating on the aforestated theory.

After ceaseless quarrels, domestic and wild animals agreed to sign a peace treaty to stem the ongoing massacre of each other. According to the treaty, all animals are equal and should live as 'brothers' and 'sisters'. The signing ceremony was to take place at noon, near the central watering hole at the heart of the scenic Amboseli National Park, Kenya – See Appendix 3. By ten o'clock, the venue was busting at the seams. There were congratulations, and brotherly shaking of paws/hooves/feet.

The Steering Committee - the lion (convenor), the bull (co-convenor), the elephant, the hen, the crocodile, the donkey, the butterfly, the goldfish and some other notables spoke one after another in exciting terms about the object of the peace treaty. Everyone was joyful!

Thereafter, notable virtuosos played varying instruments: the antelope - drums; the cat – xylophone; the monkey – flute; the duck – *kayamba*; the praying mantis - guitar. Fascinating vocals courtesy of the humming bird, the rabbit, the horse and the porcupine completed the orchestra. The ostrich, the peacock, the pig, the giraffe and the hippopotamus, all excellent dancers, had great success entertaining their colleagues.

After several other dancers, the billy goat dizzily jumped into the middle and, by his clumsiness, caused a certain amount of disorder. For some reason, Billy's dancing style caught the hyena's ever-calculating eye. He moved nearer pretending to admire Billy's dancing moves. Finally, he could no longer contain himself - he threw himself brutally onto Billy and tightly planted his sharp teeth on the neck's soft muscles. Billy cried-out wildly for help. No one bothered!

Chaos ensued... The leopard chopped-off a sizable chunk of the sheep's derrière while the jackal maniacally pursued the expectant pig. The members of the Steering Committee vainly tried to restore order. Instead, the lion tore-off one of the bull's ear. In retaliation, the bull gouged-out his fellow co-convenor's left eye.

The brawl spread like a bushfire. At the end, there was a generalized escape - domestic animals, instinctively, headed towards the nearby Kimana Village, pursued by the bloodthirsty wild beasts. The peace treaty failed!

[This story cleverly captures how the opposing political elites in the *Fortress in a once Seemingly Peaceful Realm* consistently fail to reach at even the simplest agreement at the expense of the voiceless/powerless Africans].

In a similar fashion, once the official power in human dealings is lost, tumult becomes a regular engagement, which threatens public peace. To paraphrase Martin Luther King Junior (1929-68), nothing renders a society as frightening as when the street mobs claim justice from the authorities. This brings us to the day I was walking to work at an international casino in Nairobi – soon after my first academic degree – See Appendix 3.

At Kimathi Street-Kenyatta Avenue Junction, a sharp shriek pierced the air: *Mwizi! Mwizi!* (Thief! Thief!). A middle-aged woman chased after a relatively younger man who, in his state of drunkenness, was doing more stumbling over his feet than running. The cry transformed idlers, pedestrians, hawkers, drivers, passengers and random strangers into a hysterical mob. They got riled-up once they saw the cellular phone, evidence of the man's crime. They punched, kicked, bludgeoned and stoned the suspect. Rolled into a foetal position, he screamed for help.

Watching this, my throat tightened as dark memories of Charles' being beaten criss-crossed my mind - remember Charles' beating detailed earlier? As if re-living that devastating episode, *tears flowed freely from some inextinguishable source of sadness. It made me both angry and irritated.* At the same time, I recited my *Life Lesson*: *For the love of humanity… refuse indifference as an option to violence.* I begged the crowd to stop the beating and instead we take the man to the nearby police station. With that, the riotous crowd declared me an accomplice of the robber, and ordered me to remain silent or otherwise I get the same treatment – mob (in)justice. My resolve to stop the beating abruptly ended when I was hit with sizable rock at the back of my head, sending me into a free-fall.

Before I touched the ground, the beating of the stealer re-commenced. Suddenly, two men appeared from nowhere – one carrying two old car tyres and the other one with a jerrycan full of petrol, shouting: *Weka tairi! Weka tairi!*

[*Weka tairi* is also referred to as necklacing. In this genre of mob-punishment a suspect is tied-up, encased in a stack of used car tyres, doused with petrol and set-on fire. The irate mob only leaves once the culprit is reduced to ashes or police officers appear.]

On hearing this new call, the enfeebled victim summoned his energy and convinced the unruly mob to listen to him. He looked at the two men, drew his left-hand middle finger-up and menacingly asked them: *what wrong with you maniacs? You find us doing our thing 'peacefully', then you start your foolishness of weka tairi! People of good will, ignore these hooligans! Let us continue with what we were doing… continue beating me up… no necklacing here!* Do you see the irony of the thief's disheartening plea? Sadly, the young man was burnt to death. And, from that experience, I can assure you dear reader, one never forgets the piercing screams of a dying man or the acrid smell of burning human flesh.

This is just to reiterate that, at times I get a feeling that some fellow humans are excited by raw violence. In the frenzy of violence – a hat is stolen: *kill the thief*; a bus is involved in an accident: *stone the driver to death*; a boy dies in a hospital: *lynch the grandmother for she is a witch*; the *matatu*/bus conductor is smelly: *throw him into the river*; a beautiful woman appears in public alone: *strip her naked*. What absurdity?

Again, some worthwhile digression. A day after the lynching of the young man, I recounted the story to my lovely mother. Just like when I was eleven-year-old, after Charles' beating, she touched my fresh wound at the back of my head and said:

> Son, I am happy for your courageous movement of love; for your spontaneous act of compassion. You found yourself in a situation that you felt was wrong. You stepped in and went against the crowd; to fight for what is right; to go against the grain of injustice. You were good without knowing, as you acted impulsively. Remember: a good deed is never so good as when the doer is unaware that he is doing good. You did a good deed unselfconsciously... I am proud of you son!

My mother's vast faith in me gives me the nerve to try what my own inclination often resists. For she makes me feel several inches taller. Through her, I have learnt to trust in the love and the example of others: that we are made for each other and born for the good of the whole. For, her worldview moves beyond an ethnic-based understanding of humanity towards an ethic of mutuality and interdependence. She believes that like a butterfly effect, whatever happens in the Africa's remotest corner, impacts the rest of the continent for good or ill.

Dealing with violence

How can Africans tackle a gigantic social issue such as violence? Foremost, they need to acknowledge that everyone has innate greatness ready to be extracted. They should hold themselves to a higher standard in all their undertakings. Both individually and collectively, they must decide that, it is unacceptable for any African to suffer in the hands of another being. Then, they must believe that everyone has a responsibility to make a lasting positive difference – see little *Kolibri*'s story in Chapter 4.

Behaviourists propose that, countering violence should begin at early stages of life. In this case, child behaviour management techniques of praising the behaviour one wants to see should be used here. However, this needs to start at a young age when parents play a pivotal role in their children's lives. Behavioural modelling of Africa's children does not stop with the parents though. The entire society must play an active role as information technology has overhauled the way people interact with each other. If well used, role modelling-oriented socialisation can propagate expected behaviour.

Through this model, if the adults who the youngsters are expected to admire and imitate are consistently respectful and fair to them, they ultimately accept this as the normal way of relating to others – being courteous and looking for compromise. Similarly, if those in authority over the youngsters are violent and abusive towards them, then this becomes normal for the youth. This is referred to as normalisation of violence as necessary and justified means of resolving conflicts. They reproduce this violence in their relationships with others. Put differently, they become socialised, through imitation, into repression and violent means to achieve their desired ends.

As mentioned elsewhere in this book, there are a myriad of reasons leading to violence: mental illness, diminishing income, alcohol and drug intake, and the breakdown of the traditional African family. These are irrefutable reasons. To create a sustainable change for a violent person, there must be a change in 'identity'. This is the only way to produce a consistent change in the acquired behaviour.

In 2006, for instance, I briefly worked with an anti-violence organization in Bangkok, Thailand, assisting selected locals to discard their 'violent behaviour'. This work was premised on the fact that, there are people who have survived the ravages of alcohol and drug abuse, who have lost their jobs, and who have never experienced a stable family life – yet, they never resorted to violence. The results of this work were phenomenal. One astounding example of this was a middle-aged man named Sunan. Through a six month tailor-made program, we helped him make shifts in his beliefs, which enabled him to develop strategies to support his 'new identity'. Today, Sunan is not only out of gangsterism and off-drugs, but he is also responsible and a contributor to his community - he is a public bus driver.

In interviewing people involved in all sorts of violence, I have realised that many of them are just like Sunan. Their overriding challenges are not different from those we experience in our daily lives. Nonetheless, they have values that preclude a change; guided by rules that prevent them from moving forward, while their 'artificial' identity ties them to their limiting circumstances. With concerted efforts from us all, we can be the bridge between the harsh reality of violence and the challenge of personal responsibility that rejoining non-violent society requires. Above all, a violent person needs to know that someone cares about him and is committed to offering him strategies that will steer his life in a new direction. Unquestioningly, not all violent individuals are ready for change, but those who are clearly deserve our support. Throughout the process, we all need to keep in mind: small efforts can make a big difference.

Concluding remarks

If your tradition requires you to be violent against another being, you need a new tradition. It is imbecility of tremendous proportions to hoard mediocre traditions, which imprison you to rigid rules of a self-observed inward-looking society. For traditions are supposed to be guideposts that help us counter alienation and confusion. They define who we are.

Nonetheless, if there is violence in public, there is no guarantee that there is no violence in the private domain. In this journey of going *Beyond Negative Ethnicity, Corruption and Violence* we call it *domestic violence: the frontline of war against humanity.*

CHAPTER 6

Domestic Violence: The Frontline of War against Humanity

See what you make me do?

Yesterday, I loved him.
As he claim'd to love me.
Today, his presence reeks of lifeless dust.
E'en darkness can't fight him off.
He has no rhyme!
As he's a poorly written song,
Whose bold melody clashes.
He crawls not to scream,
And, he's ne'er slow to hit.
Yet, he shamelessly screams at me:
See what you make me do?

Yesterday, he claim'd to love me.
Today, he tighten'd his hands around my throat.
Stealin' the light out of my eyes;
And, thievin' my strength to stand-tall.
Yet, he shamelessly scream'd at me:
See what you made me do?

Today, my silence cries.
My third degree burns on my heart sob; and,
My wounds on my soul weep.
My fearsome nights cripple my cerebral cortex.
Yet, he ceaselessly screams at me:
See what you make/made me do?

Preamble

In concurrence with Chapter 5, this chapter takes into cognisance the fact that domestic violence (DV) affects both women and men. *The U.S. National Family Violence Survey* conducted by Straus and Gelles in 1975 presented the earliest empirical evidence that women perpetrate DV at roughly the same rate as men. The survey found that 12% of both men and women had experienced some kind of DV in the last twelve months. In 1990, another U.S. study, *the National Comorbidity Survey*, found a similar trend: 18% of men and 17% of women had experienced DV. In England and Wales, *The 1995 Home Office Research Study*, revealed that in the twelve months prior to the survey, 4% of both men and women had been assaulted by an intimate. In 2000, *The Canadian General Social Survey* found that from 1994 to 1999, 4% of both men and women had experienced DV in a relationship in which they were still involved. A similar trend was uncovered in 2005 through *The Canadian General Social Survey*, which found that 4% of men and 3% of women had experienced DV in a relationship in which they were still involved.

Reviews of publications in the *Journal of Violence and Victims; Journal of Trauma Violence Abuse*; and, *Journal of Aggression and Violent Behaviour*, from 2008 to 2018, show that although minor DV is equal for both genders, more severe violence is perpetrated by men. They reveal that women's DV is more likely motivated by anger, a need for attention, or as a response to their partner's own violence while men's is more likely motivated by need to control. Further, they indicate that men are more likely to beat up, choke or strangle their partners; while women are more likely to use objects to harm their partner, slap, kick, bite or punch.

For both male and female victims of DV, the negative effects range from depression, anxiety and low self-esteem to troubled personal relationships. It also leads to the development of a victim mentality, which plays a vital role in re-victimization. This can result in suicide or attempt at suicide.

VIOLENCE AGAINST WOMEN IN PRIVATE AND PUBLIC DOMAINS

The axe forgets what the tree remembers.
(African Proverb)

During my over twenty years conducting social science studies, I have interviewed thousands of women throughout the world – Africa, Asia, Australasia, Caribbean, Middle-East, North America and South America. More than 60% of them have experienced at least one incident of physical or sexual violence since the age of sixteen.

Flowing from the above therefore, I declare that violence against women knows no cultural, religious, class, or geographical boundaries. It affects women in developed as well as in developing countries. This type of violence manifests itself in different forms: kidnapping of school girls; forced child marriages; female genital mutilation; and, violence by intimate partners. Concerning the last form of violence, Veronic from Cape Town, South Africa (Appendix 2), observes:

> I got married at the age of sixteen. We had it so good, but my husband beat me regularly. He would beat me about why he did not make more money. He had multiple sexual partners and came home late and drunk. He would leave and not come back for weeks. When he re-appeared, he would cry on his knees telling me how much he loves me and cares for our family. Naively, I would accept his crude apologies.
>
> There were so many changes in him, including in bed; he seemed sexually metamorphosed; would try many funny and sophisticated sex styles – doggie style and the cowgirl are among the less crazy ones. Before, there was no foreplay prior

to having sex. Towards the end of our time together, he would literally burry his head in me..., you know, down there – in my private parts. He called it pussy-eating. *[She smiles shyly, blushing a little]*. He did alien things in the name of sex that you would not normally do with your wife. At the end, I became pregnant again.

Nevertheless, the beatings continued. At my sixth month of pregnancy, he kicked me badly on the tummy. I developed medical-related problems, which I thought would disappear as usual. At around midnight, I started to have premature labour pains. Our neighbour took me to the nearby health clinic, as my husband had not come back from his drinking binge. I was in the emergency room for half an hour and the night-nurse delivered my underweight baby-boy. Sadly, he only lived for three hours. To cap it all, my husband abandoned us, leaving me with our other three-year-old son to care for.

Violence against women in *the Fortress in a once Seemingly Peaceful Realm* and elsewhere in Africa also rears its ugly head in the public domain. To qualify the foregoing, I share a quick but piteous story.

One sunny Saturday afternoon in May 2018, together with my social science research assistant, we were having a drink in a bar-beer along Maria Mutola Avenue in Maputo, Mozambique – See Appendix 2. Through the window, I could see a beautiful, virginal-looking girl in her early twenties wearing tight-fitting pants standing at the bus station across the busy road. Half a dozen young men approached her wanting to know why she was 'indecently dressed'. Like wild dogs on a hunting spree, they descended on her with obscenities, kicks and punches before stripping her naked. The harassment continued until two uniformed police officers arrested the unfortunate woman.

Life has a way of testing our commitment to our values. My test came when the three of the six perpetrators came to the bar where I was. They were openly proud of their accomplishment, which thoroughly displeased me. Quick confession: at times of injustice of this mammoth proportion, I get completely disconnected to self – fear evaporates while courage solidifies; the need to support the status quo vanishes while the urge of fairness kicks-in; apathy disappears while empathy sets-in; and, hatred dissolves while love intensifies then solidifies.

Questions raced through my tormented head: *What should I do? Should I confront these hooligans? Should I walk up to their table, stand there and just stare at them?* I was not proud of these questions as their responses had the potential of igniting more violence. In a moment, I took my old notebook, the one with my *Life Lesson*, from my breast pocket. I read the front page: *For the love of humanity, have no moral middle ground and refuse indifference as an option to violence. Be unyielding and inflexible in its opposition. Be intelligent! Make a difference...* I paused. Then, unfamiliar sensation, as adrenaline flew through my blood stream like a faucet turned on high making my skin tingle, took over me.

Unhesitatingly, through my able research assistant, I invited the three mean-looking men to our table. An invitation they excitedly honoured for they were assured of a free beer supply. In the next sixty-three minutes, the three self-appointed moral guardians discussed the reasoning behind what they had just done – stripped naked a helpless woman in public.

Dressing scantily is uncivilized behaviour. It disturbs public order and tarnishes women's honour and respect. It tempts men and on some occasions leads to traffic accidents. What did she want to show us? [*They asked themselves*]. We stripped her naked to see what she wanted us to see. [*They answered their fatuous question then burst into loud obnoxious laughter*]. She rightfully got what she deserved with her provocative dressing. [*They concluded with a sense of importance*].

Whenever, I attempted to question their warped logic, they reacted violently with their middle fingers drawn-up and warned me that if I continued, they would send me back to Kenya in a coffin. It was a textbook example that you only get into trouble if you try to counsel a fool. A pure demonstration of the futility of trying to teach a pig how to sing; it wastes your time and it irritates the pig. I wasted my time and irritated the goons. For, there was a dark void in their understanding; they were a people whose bodies moved while their minds slept. Like a child banging its tiny fragile head on a floor in tantrum, they were oblivious of the sheer inanity of their actions and the consequences of their destructive acts. Anyhow, even in a stressful and unpredictable environment, I lived by what I believed was right – *to have no moral middle ground and to refuse indifference as an option to violence.* To me, nothing in life can match the fulfilment of knowing you have done what you truly believe is right.

Nonetheless, I have never understood the wisdom of arresting the woman by the two law-enforcers. Is it not double punishment? Is it not like condemning a robbed woman because her possession of money precipitated the evil act of robbery? In my opinion, any civilized society must protect the robbed and punish the robber. We must overhaul any system, which overly protects the rights of criminals while leaving the innocent victims of crime without justice. For, a misguided society bears the guilt of crimes committed in hopeless situations.

To me it is treating symptoms rather than the cause of the social malaise. It is like this imaginary fellow who stood on the banks of a river. Suddenly, he sees someone caught in the raging current, bounced about on the jagged rocks, and hears him calling for help. He leaps in, pulls the drowning man to safety, gives him mouth-to-mouth resuscitation, attends to the man's wounds, and calls for medical help. As he sits to catch his breath, he hears two more screams emanating from the same spot of the river. Again, he jumps in and makes another daring rescue, this time of two young women. Before he even has a chance to think, he hears four more people calling for help. Soon the man is exhausted, and yet fresh screams continued. If only he had taken the time to travel a short distance upstream, he could have discovered who was throwing these people into the river. He could have saved all his efforts by addressing the cause of the problem rather than its effects. For when we eliminate the cause, the symptoms evaporate. Otherwise, we will be doing the same thing over and over again and expecting different results.

Differently put, instead of playing the Good Samaritan on life's roadside, this imaginary fellow should strive to transform the whole Jericho Road so that users are not constantly beaten and robbed as they make their journey on life's highway. In any case, true compassion is more than flinging coins to beggars; rather, it is restructuring the system that manufactures mendicants – see also Chapter 4. Consequently, I challenge you dear reader to play your part towards a sustained transformation of those notorious Jericho Roads in Abuja, Accra, Algiers, Brazzaville, Cairo, Conakry, Dakar, Pretoria, Kinshasa, Maputo, Nairobi and elsewhere in *the Fortress in a once Seemingly Peaceful Realm* – See Appendix 2. Unsafe 'roads' where people knock each other down and no one stops to pick them up. For, both individually and collectively, we feed *The Violence-spitting Vipers* that reside within and without ourselves.

Parents are their children's primary models

Through my many and varied social science studies, I have realized that sexual-psychological stereotyping of females begins when the physician announces: it is a girl! And, that pronouncement has consequences for both men and women. For the reality is that in some cases, the girl is not allowed to be born. If she is born, her survival is not guaranteed. If she survives, she does not get the status she deserves - equal to that of a boy.

In Africa, gender inequality is apparent in many spheres of life: politics, religion and the workplace. In varying degrees, both men and women receive blatant and/or covert messages, that boys are more important than girls. This fabricated inequality creates a rationale for humiliation, intimidation, control, abuse, and even killing. It instils an erroneous and self-serving belief that men have a divine right to be in-charge and to control women.

This mind-set begets violence against women and girls. It excuses parents who decide to abort a female embryo; the family that chooses to educate a boy above a girl; parents who expect girls to stay home to take care of the family; the brutal husband who beats his wife; and/or, the employer who has a lower pay scale for female employees.

As a people, Africans should never ignore what lessons their children will carry with them about their gender and self-worth. They should endeavour to teach their girls to worry less about fitting into glass slippers and more about shattering glass ceilings.

Parents are their children's safety nets, and their primary models of empathy and self-respect. Coming together as families and concerned adults to out-rightly deal with DV against women therefore, will have far-reaching positive impacts. In any case, for every moment Africans remain silent, they conspire against their women; and, for every woman denied an opportunity to fulfil her potential, the continent destroys a generation. In other words, as long as a society prevents women from making a meaningful contribution to its wellbeing, progress will be slow. For a society that refuses to acknowledge the equal role of more than half of itself, is doomed to failure.

Restrain from harming and hating her

A casual examination of the bottommost grassroots and the uppermost halls of power in *the Fortress in a Seemingly Peaceful Realm* reveals that many people embrace the ideology of social suppression. A type of suppression that delivers overt and/or covert messages about being a good girl – 'staying in control'. It directly and/or indirectly teaches her that 'going out of control' drives others away. To 'stay in control' therefore, she must limit her feelings and check her primal energy. As a result, she suppresses her inherent potential. Hence, the patriarchal society, as currently practised in Africa, robs the girl of her innate power. The power to choose; to create; and, to freely will each moment of her existence. To exhale, she needs to fight!

In the context of this book, nonviolence against women means avoiding not only physical but also psychological violence. This way, you not only stop harming her, but you also restrain from hating her for who she is. Hence, it is imperative for all Africans to extend their stand against violence to teaching their children a broader definition of humanity that entails being empathetic, caring and loving.

Unquestioningly, there is a major change on this front throughout *the Fortress in a Seemingly Peaceful Realm*. And, it is not just because of new laws. It has taken a drastic shift in societal attitudes about how the people view sexual violence, and how much they value the dignity of their grandmothers, mothers, wives, sisters, aunts, nieces, daughters and granddaughters.

Nonetheless, it is up to all Africans to maintain this momentum, as the best indicator of an individual's character is how he treats people who cannot fight back. In line with the foregoing therefore, the gravity of sexist vitriol directed at some female (political) leaders mystifies me to unimaginable extent. Further, political success by known misogynists throughout the globe convinces me that there is an affective dynamic to politics and an emotional narrative that makes sense in an alternate universe from which I am functionally excluded.

Such (political) success proves that it is easy to hate and difficult to love. But then, this is how the general scheme of things works. All good things are difficult to achieve; and bad things are easy to get. Conversely, the ancient and inexhaustible law dictates: only love dispels hate. Thence, speak and act with a pure mind and a loving heart; and, happiness will follow as your shadow, unshakable.

Misogyny is destructive to the spirit of a society

Misogyny has the potential to push women into the self-destructive mind-set of victimhood. In such a mind-set, rather than emphasizing on their strength or inner worth, the aggrieved emphasize their social marginalization. Thus, sexism and misogyny are destructive to the spirit of a society. All Africans should therefore reject them and let women know that they collectively have their back. They are ready to protect their rights, as that is what a civilized society stands for.

However, bringing about social change is a life-long undertaking. Thus, to transform *the Fortress in a once Seemingly Peaceful Realm* into a community that African women deserve, everyone has to get up every day ready for the fight. For the battle for fairness and decency starts afresh each day. Africans should be prepared for whatever comes their way, and that includes failure. This should not be a new lesson for anyone; it is a fact of life. For, it is always easier to move forward with the wind at your back than it is to advance into a strong headwind.

When girls are respected, they become empowered women. They break the chain of poverty and fuel the national/continental growth as freedom from DV is the ground rule for active participation in a society. This argument is premised by a higher form of masculinity that sees women as people for whom violence means infringement of basic human rights and deprivation of full potential.

When women are respected, their beauty radiates effortlessly. That beauty can only be seen through her eyes. For, that is the gateway to her heart. The place where absolute love and unadulterated beauty reside. Moreover, it is only with the heart that one can see rightly as what is essential is invisible to the eye. For her inner beauty to shine therefore, you need to touch her golden soul with appreciation and respect. Thus, look into her soul not her blouse.

In a nutshell, be reminded: each time you stand up for the improvement of women's lives, you send forth unending ripples of hope. Ripples that criss-cross each other from multiple centres of energy creating a wave capable of tearing-down the mightiest walls of oppression and misogyny. To bring this *Section* to a closure therefore, I invite all Africans to be the candles that generate the light of respect for women. In case you are unable to be that candle, then be the mirror that reflects that light; for, a woman brought you into this world and therefore you have no right to disrespect one.

DOMESTIC VIOLENCE AGAINST MEN TAKES MANY FORMS

When violence enters the house,
Love leaves through the chimney.
(Turkish Proverb)

A review of over 30 refereed articles in the *Journal of Violence and Victims*; *Journal of Trauma Violence Abuse*; and, *Journal of Aggression and Violent Behaviour*, from 2008 to 2018, shows that the rate of assault by women on male partners is about the same as the rate of assault by men on their female partners. Nonetheless, women are three times more likely as men to use weapons when attacking their partners. Thus, a greater proportion of male victims sustain physical injuries. Additionally, these injuries are more extensive than those suffered by female victims.

Contrastingly, there is a notion that because men are (generally) physically stronger than women, that they cannot be victims of DV. In reality, DV is not about strength, but rather the intention behind it. Consequently, DV against men comes in all shapes and forms: emotional torture, sexual abuse, physical maltreatment and verbal threats. Due to brevity of space, I only share Job, Brian, Youssef and Diop's stories. The four were randomly selected from a pool of 157 male participants in *Focus Group* discussions on DV in Africa. Of importance to note, this author has vast data related to DV in the continent courtesy of the ongoing longitudinal research on social life in Africa. This study covers the eleven countries shown in Appendix 2.

Job is a sous-chef in a two-star hotel in the outskirts of Durban, South Africa – See Appendix 2. He lives with his wife and five children in Sydenham, a middle-scale neighbourhood. Job notes:

My wife has been physically and verbally abusing me for over a decade. She hits me with all types of objects. She slaps, kicks, claws and bites me in the presence of our five children. I silently endure her mood swings and predilection to violence whenever things do not go her way. Ignoring her anger tantrum only worsens the situation. I am her punching bag!

I know this might sound ironical or even outright stupid, but I see no way out of this quagmire for me. I am stuck. I have to live with it. I am powerless, and that feeling is my prison. I entered of my own free will, I locked the door, and threw the key into the sea.

In the beginning, I thought that acting violently was her way to express herself. I wanted to give her space to grow. To be a first rate version of herself, not a second rate version of someone else. Paradoxically, by the time I realised she was abusing me, I was too ashamed to talk about it with anyone. Today, as I talk to you, I fear to be ridiculed and stigmatised as women beating men is unimaginable in my Zulu culture.

Job's case proves that male victims of DV are often judged harshly for 'allowing' themselves to be beaten by women. This view is based upon the assumption that men are physically stronger than women, and, therefore, are expected to suppress any form of female aggression. The entire reasoning disregards the fact that violent women tend to use objects during DV at a higher rate than violent men.

In worst-case scenario, men victims are treated as out-casts by the entire society. To exemplify the foregoing, I detail Brian's quandary. Brian is a middle-level manager in an international clearing and forwarding company based in Industrial Area, Nairobi, Kenya - See Appendix 3. He lives in the up-scale neighbourhood of Hurlingham with his wife and two daughters. Brian believes he has seen and experienced the worst form of DV. He says:

My wife is a devil incarnate. She punches and slaps me any time we have a slight disagreement. Then, she would apologise profusely. It is literally like a flick of a switch, she goes from extremely angry, horrific and violent, to lovely, calm and apologetic. Within no time, the cycle of violence would repeat itself. It is difficult to understand but I love her; I love her so much that I do not want to hurt her. I do not want to raise my hand to her.

One Friday night we went out to drink beer. On our way home, we got into an argument on a very petty issue: who consumed more beer that evening. My wife hit me on the face with her handbag thereby breaking my nose. She continued kicking me despite my effort to calm her down.

Her screams called the attention of two well-built men who were passing by. Without inquiring what was happening, they punched and stomped on me. They then escorted her to our apartment leaving me lying unconscious on the cold street. I found myself at Kenyatta National Hospital the following morning with a broken nose, two fractured ribs and multiple cuts on my face.

After my discharge from the hospital, I went to the police station to report my mistreatment. Unbelievably, the police officers were unwilling to pursue my case. They called me a henpecked social misfit. Due to persistent ridicule by my relatives, friends and colleagues at work, I dropped the charges. Despite the unabated daily abuse, I am still married to her for the sake of our two young daughters.

The uncaring reaction by Brian's relatives, friends, colleagues and the law-enforcers affirms African society's misplaced expectation of a man. He must be strong – whatever that implies; never breaks down and never cries. He must lead and provide for his family. He is judged as a failure if not a social misfit for any slight negative deviation from this rigid societal expectation.

Nonetheless, I will never forget Youssef's predicament. He lives in a two bed-roomed apartment in Nigeria's coastal City of Lagos with his youthful wife – see Appendix 2. I let Youssef share his story.

I met my wife at the university. At the beginning, we were happily married. After one year, she mutated into a monster! According to her, she gets sexual satisfaction whenever she physically abuses me – a reasoning I fail to understand. She slaps, punches, canes and hurls me onto the sofa. Early this year, I suffered a horrible concussion after she hit me on the forehead with a plank of firewood.

Her violence of choice is manhandling my private parts. She firmly holds my manhood then literally pulls me around the house. She enjoys my screaming and begging for mercy. My screams set her into a state of ecstasy. In her words, that gives her multiple orgasms. She turns wild, slaps and hits me with whatever object her hands land on.

To counter the unceasing abuse, I slowly drifted into alcoholism. At times, I am drunk 24 hours a day, seven days a week. In that state, I am physically weak and therefore, I cannot effectively counteract her sadistic deeds. She takes full advantage of my inability to defend myself.

One Sunday, in February 2017, after two hours of an excruciating session of manhandling of my manhood, my wife chopped-it off with a kitchen knife. I fainted. She took me to a local health centre for re-attachment. She insisted to be present as I talked to the physician. I vaguely told the doctor what had been happening - that I am injured, depressed and my wife is threatening to leave me. The doctor mocked and laughed at me before organizing for a surgical procedure.

As in the Job and Brian cases, Youssef could not openly admit to being a victim of female perpetrated DV. For him and many men, such an admission is a proof of submission to a female partner and an abandonment of the veneer of machismo, which African societies do not expect from them.

Reasons why women assault their male partners

In no specific order and without going into details, here are the nine most common reasons given by female respondents for being aggressive towards their male partners. These reasons are lifted from over 30 refereed articles alluded to earlier in this Chapter.

- ❖ I believe women are in charge in a domestic situation and have a right to strike their (male) partners if they break set rules.
- ❖ I admire empowered women in the movies and on television who hit their (male) partners.
- ❖ I believe it is important and healthy for women to express anger physically particularly in an intimate relationship.
- ❖ I am turned on sexually whenever I am physically aggressive towards my intimate partner.
- ❖ I have always admired my mother for her physical aggressiveness towards my father. I want to be like her.
- ❖ I was always physically aggressive towards my brother and he never fought back. Further, I have found that men do not hit women and therefore I am not fearful of retaliation from my man.
- ❖ I believe if there is true gender equality, women should be able to express their anger physically at men.
- ❖ I feel empowered when I am aggressive towards my partner.
- ❖ I want to engage my partner emotionally.

The attempt by some women to use physical aggression to re-establish emotional contact with their male partners mystifies me to the core. For, it is an act of the unwise to use violence to achieve a beneficial end such as improved verbal and/or emotional communication.

Ambivalence on domestic violence against men

Clearly, the justice system world-over heavily focuses on the plight of women. Studies show that women who assault their male partners are less likely to be arrested than men who attack their female partners. Further, law enforcement agencies and the court system view female perpetrators of DV as victims rather than offenders. Thus, men fear that if they report their sufferings to the police, they will be assumed to be the aggressor, and be arrested.

The U.S. National Family Violence Survey, mentioned in the introduction of this Chapter validates the foregoing. The Study found that:

- When a woman called the police to report DV, the man was ordered out of the house in 41% of cases; when a man called, the woman was ordered out of the house in 0% of cases.
- When a woman called, the man was threatened with immediate arrest in 28% of cases; when a man called, the woman was threatened with arrest in 0% of cases.
- When a woman called, the man was arrested in 15% of cases; when a man called, the woman was arrested in 0% of cases.

In fact, in 12% of the cases, when the man called, the man himself was arrested. This was the case with Diop, a 34-year-old truck-driver living in Hann Estate in Dakar, Senegal - See Appendix 2. His wife consistently abused him. When he called the police officers to their matrimonial home, she lied that she was the actual victim. The officers arrested and charged Diop in the court of law for instigating DV. His poor family struggled to raise money for an attorney and he was acquitted for lack of evidence.

The number of male victims in Africa is likely to be greater than law enforcement statistics suggest as men are often more reluctant than women to report their abuse or seek help when they are the victims of DV. This reluctance is due to a number of reasons:

- ❖ Domestic violence against men is generally less recognized by African societies than violence against women.
- ❖ Fear of people saying that the woman is the actual victim, and that she was acting in self-defence.
- ❖ Africa's open socio-cultural stereotypes of masculinity: this results in social stigma regarding the male victims' perceived lack of machismo and other denigrations of their masculinity.

Underreporting of male-oriented DV compromises effective intervention

Like their female counterparts, male victims of DV suffer trauma, which includes but is not limited to: anxiety, depression, loss of self-esteem and emotional desensitization. They also face stigmatization, isolation and abandonment by family members as well as by the public. Some male victims end-up abusing alcohol and drugs - see for example Youssef's story discussed elsewhere.

Incontestably, underreporting is a significant impediment to effective intervention. It severely impairs the understanding of this social phenomenon. Adequate reporting would provide the necessary evidence for a shift in policy and legislative frameworks. Currently, they blatantly fail to protect male victims of DV.

For individual survivors, this collective failure leads to a lack of assistance and/or justice. As *the Fortress in a once Seemingly Peaceful Realm* moves forward to address this issue however, the society needs to take care not to inadvertently harm other vulnerable groups in the process. Psychosocial strategies aimed at the specific needs of male survivors for instance, must be carefully designed to avoid unintentional reinforcement of male dominance over women.

Concluding remarks

Africans must keep reminding their (young) men to show women the respect they deserve. They must remind them of the need to be outraged by any form of sexual assault; and to do their part unprompted to stop it from happening. Families and communities should create a social situation where every young male experiences positive peer pressure in terms of how he is supposed to treat girls and women.

In a similar manner, women have a critical role to play in supporting the societal shift advocated for in this Chapter. They need to be at the core of the conversation. They need to speak-out in support of gender equality. And, importantly, they need to be proud in identifying themselves as masculinists.

I dream thus, of a future where both boys and girls will be free to live-out their individual dreams. Why? Because,

For e'ery girl who's tired of being labell'd over-sensiti'e;
There's a boy who fears to be gentle.
For e'ery strong girl who's tired of actin' weak;
There's a vulnerable boy tired of appearin' strong.

In closing therefore, Africans should never stay silent on issues of disrespect to men and/or women. For it is misguided to highlight other social challenges like negative ethnicity and corruption and then mention disrespect for fellow beings as a footnote. For, national attention is a zero-sum game. A game that remains incomplete without an in-depth scrutiny of *political violence in Africa*.

CHAPTER 7

Political violence in Africa

The unwisers

Africa's soul's in flames!
No more birds of the sky.
For, nak'd 'n petulant men freely hover in the air,
Disguis'd as leaders.
With this dent'd common decency,
The livin' competes with the dead.
They wish ill to the depart'd soul.
As they're disjoint'd, toxic 'n full of myopic imaginings.

Fools learn not.
For, knowledge cleaves their brains makin' them duller.
They fight for positions o'er people.
Look at my look!
Such is their raw swellin' pride.
As they compete with the deceas'd!

O' the unwisers!
They're strand'd on the side of the riverbank.
Like true maniacs, they run up-and-down.
Unable to cross the rivulet.
For, they can't see beyond the beginnin'.
Thus, where'er they live,
There's catastrophic tragedy.
As, they're vipers,
That grow in size 'n ne'er in wisdom.

Preamble

Political violence in *the Fortress in a once Seemingly Peaceful Realm* is not prepared in sordid dens of crime. Rather, it is conceived and ordered in aerated, well-lighted and carpeted boardrooms. Such violence-related motions are moved, seconded and carried by quiet men with white collars and smooth-shaven cheeks who do not need to raise their voices. For, all wars begin in the hearts of men, not on battlefields. Outside those boardrooms, political violence creates unimaginable levels of sufferings for the victims, the perpetrators, the families and the general society.

To comprehend political violence's wide-ranging consequences, we need to think of any African society as consisting of various but inter-connected strands like a spider's web – alone the stand is weak. Conversely, when interwoven and inter-dependent, it becomes strong. Consequently, when there is a problem in the web, perhaps within a family, the whole web must be restructured to maintain its harmony, strength and general vitality. Otherwise put, you cannot remove/add a piece from/to the web without altering the whole. It follows from this that all political players must work together for the sake of cohesion in the society.

Elections and political violence

Elections are the means by which Africans choose their leaders thereby expressing preference for given policies. By voting, Africans add their voice to the chorus that forms the basis for action.

Chorus for action

By votin',
You add your voice to the chorus.
A chorus that forms the basis for national action.
It breathes life into the principle of the consent of the govern'd.
As it's fundamental in any democracy;
And, a civic sacrament:
The highest civic responsibility Africans have.

Elections facilitate change in leadership in a structured, transparent and legal manner. In such a competitive process, tension is inevitable and even desirable to the extent that it can bring out the best of the participants. Thus, in many cases, elections enhance democracy and its institutions.

Elections can also degenerate into violence. This happens when contestants breach set rules or fail to accept the outcomes as the legitimate expression of the will of the populace.

Uncontestably though, elections are not the sole cause of pre- or post-election violence in Africa. For, links between elections, peace and the democratization process are contingent upon innumerable external factors. They only provide the opportunity for people to express grievances related to underlying ills: unfair resource allocation, social injustice, marginalization and ethnic mistrust. These real or perceived social issues arise from reasons beyond the scope of this modest work. Nevertheless, it is accurate to note that in spite of the ascendance of the democratization process across *the Fortress in a once Seemingly Peaceful Realm*, political violence is on the rise. This concretizes the other social malaise we have examined so far – negative ethnicity, corruption and domestic violence.

As practised currently, political competition in Africa is not about serving the people. The principal actors are contesting for fame, power and wealth accumulation. As a result, the continent competes at the level of scoundrel versus scoundrel. In this set-up, sycophants in the name of agents approach wealthy politicians with all forms of flattery. In return, they get some 'tea' and/or other forms of refreshments and small amounts of cash. The act would then be splashed in the local media. The politician basks in applause, while agents spend the small donations on themselves, and the bilateral cycle is complete. The politician needs sycophants to sing their praises, and both parties barter their souls to keep genuine political transformation at bay. To win any reputation in this set up, one needs to go in for something not just extravagant but really out of the ordinary. For, it takes more than common profligacy to get a genuinely good person noticed let alone talked about.

Throughout the continent, these agents come up with creative but twisted moneymaking strategies – see for example Chapter 4. They beg money from the World Bank, the International Monetary Fund and other foreign/multi-national funders on behalf of the poor. When aid hits the central/national bank account, they quickly constitute a committee to disburse it into their pockets. A clear proof that thieves are never interested in gaining through difficult means. Nonetheless, this kind of foolishness is the first step towards failure. It breaks the code of morality and opens the doors of cruelty in a society – see for example chapters 2 and 4.

Concisely, *the Fortress in a once Seemingly Peaceful Realm* experiences disunity, division and conflicts fuelled every electioneering period by the politicians at the people's expense. Like sheep, ordinary people are transported to demonstrations and political rallies. With beautifully articulated words that stir people's appetite, these politicians offer heaven on earth. Illiteracy, diseases, anger, unemployment and general hopelessness are exploited with clever provocative political slogans.

Repeatedly however, the promised (national) cake is gobbled and digested even before it is fully baked by those elected and their cronies. Only the few electorates who get privileged positions get some crumbs. The rest, with their tongues cut-off and therefore rendered voiceless, board a train ended nowhere – they are used and discarded until the next electioneering period. Now they have to behave according to their conditioning – return to their hovels, save their lives and shut-up. At the end, there is a lot of tyre burning, stone throwing and screaming at rowdy demonstrations. This is what political violence in Africa is all about.

Stand up for what is right

To avoid the spectre of political violence propagated by ethnic chauvinists in *the Fortress in a once Seemingly Peaceful Realm*, Africans need to stand-up for what is right – see Chapter 2. The good must stand up to evil at all times should be the new clarion call throughout *the Fortress*. Africans must do what is right and force leaders to be accountable for their puerile utterances and primitive actions. Citizens need to be alert; to stand firm; and, to be strong against any deceitful and violent-prone manoeuvres.

True to the foregoing, one Saturday in the late 1990s, a colleague invited me to his marriage reception in his rural village several kilometres from Eldoret town, Kenya – See Appendix 3. The harsh tone of the speakers, during the speeches, made me uncomfortable. Nonetheless, I listened patiently. After the influential finished speaking and praising each other's efforts, and loud clapping and deafening choreographed ululations died out, I stood from my seat in the audience and humbly asked permission to say a few words. This caused absolute confusion for I was a non-entity – at least in the eyes of those present.

My audacity to address rich and powerful local politicians from a position of 'insignificance', released an immediate adverse reaction. Agents of the powerful hooted: *Who do you think you are? Sit down or we eject you out of here.* Somebody from the back yelled: *Let the foolish boy speak! Let us hear his bullshit!* Some people laughed; somebody roughly pushed me; I stepped forward.

All of a sudden, there was a pin drop silence. I inhaled deeply. I equivocally shared with them my idea of diversity, co-existence, mutuality and love. I slowly and clearly told them: *Telling the local young men to burn houses that belong to a certain ethnic group is an evil satisfaction.* Quarter-way through my unintentional and thus unprepared speech, the air was filled with deafening calls of: *Bunyot! Bunyot!* (Traitor! Traitor!). At the same time, a vast variety of missiles - edibles, plastic cutleries, sticks, stones, shoes and chairs -, were launched with me as their target.

Calmly and cautiously coming down from the raised platform, I looked towards my friends who had invited me to the ceremony for moral support, but they all averted their eyes. I had to take cover quickly. I was bewildered but not disgraced, as my honour has never been pegged on anyone's respect. It is based on plain truth. For freedom of truth is essential for self-respect.

For your future reference, freedom of truth is two-dimensional: freedom of choice and freedom to be yourself. It begins when you come to a point where you have no need to impress anybody. When you amass the courage to lose sight of the shore in order to cross the ocean. And, I know through experience that speaking one's truth is the most powerful tool all human beings have.

Back to the story, within a period of two weeks from that occurrence, hundreds of houses belonging to the 'offending' ethnic group were burnt, crops destroyed and livestock seized. With that, the seedling of political violence in Africa, which had been planted and sprouted in the early 1990s was watered. Its maturity phase, late 2007-early 2008, was marked by an abundance of distasteful fruits: 1,133 human deaths; 350,000 internally displaced persons; 2,000 refugees; significant numbers of sexual violence victims; and, destruction of 117,216 private properties and 491 government-owned properties - offices, vehicles, health centres and schools. Looting caused several million shillings' worth of damage. I use the example of the burning alive of my friend's one-year-old son to illustrate how the 2007-08 violence was propagated.

2007-08 post-election violence: darkest period of Kenya's history

Isaac did all types of casual labour in the outskirts of Eldoret town, Kenya - See Appendix 3. Courtesy of his dedicated work, we developed unbreakable brotherly bond. I helped him purchase a quarter-acre plot a short distance from my home. His family occupied the rooms at the back of his semi-permanent house while the front room served as a meat shop. From all standards, Isaac was doing well as he had become the go-to person for goat meat in our neighbourhood.

On Friday, 25th January 2008, in the afternoon, he left home in search of goats for the coming weekend. He returned late that day, only to find his house burnt to ashes. He had no idea where his young family was. This was at the height of 2007-08 ethnic-driven political violence in Kenya – See Appendix 2.

According to an eyewitness, all properties to be destroyed had discretely been singled-out and appropriately marked. The 'fire hooligans' would surround the identified house; break the main door; pour kerosene and/or petrol in all rooms; set fire on it; and, then stand on guard until the entire structure collapsed.

That dreadful evening, the fiendish mob barricaded all roads in that part of the town to ensure that no one escaped. Unfortunately, Isaac's wife was indoors when the hoodlums arrived at her doorstep singing war songs and brandishing all types of crude war paraphernalia. She managed to grab her two girls – six- and four-year-old. Sadly, it was too late by the time she dashed back into the furiously burning house, to pick up her one-year-old son who was deeply asleep. His miniscule body was burnt beyond recognition. The mother experienced a second-degree burn covering over 15 per cent of her body too. Her left leg had to undergo a below-knee amputation due to complications-associated with the burns.

At about midnight, Isaac joined his family at the local Chief's residence where they, together with fifty-plus others, had sought refuge. Before dawn, they were ferried to a local police station where they spent a fortnight sleeping in the cold. A few weeks later, Isaac's second born girl succumbed to pneumonia.

To shorten the long story, I talked with Isaac daily through telephone calls, emails and letters for a year – see for example Appendix 4. Today, Isaac is out of a crippling depression but suffers from post-traumatic stress disorder. He employs four people in his two small-scale businesses based in Eldoret downtown core – a taxicab and two barbershops.

The powerful exploits the powerless

In this brutish grand scheme of things, the 'powerful/privileged' exploit the 'powerless/less privileged' accurately captured by a big caricature of rats that I drew in my first year at university. I posted it strategically on walls of my university rooms throughout my fifteen years as a university student. I still have it in my private study room. It depicts a rat caught in a trap by the neck thereby leaving her butt up – totally exposed. She is evidently in shock. The first male rat is thoroughly enjoying himself from her behind. Meanwhile, two others impatiently queue for their turn behind him with satanic grins on their faces. The title of the poster vividly captures the entire barbarity – *Ain't no justice: when you are down and out, everyone wants to screw you.*

AIN'T NO JUSTICE:
When down and out
Everyone wants to screw you

The spirit of this drawing captures the essence of political violence in Africa and probably throughout the world. The agents of atrocity attack the innocent by burning their dwellings. Apparently, their fellow hoodlums are on the prowl taking advantage of the weakened prey. They go on a looting spree and raping orgy. A fresh wave of predatory goons follow, blackmailing the resigned souls with protection, treatment and provision of a combination of other necessities. For, when you are down and out, everyone wants a piece of you!

This is a confirmation that ethnic-based rifts and hatreds are born when Africans lose sight of basic humanity and fail to grasp the fact that their diversity is their strength. The rifts mature when people start fighting each other for petty ends, which distorts the noble ideals meant to further human welfare. It proves that the privileged groups seldom give up their privileges voluntarily. Individuals may see the moral light and voluntarily give up their unjust posture. But, groups tend to be more immoral than individuals. They dwell in the dark depths of prejudice instead of the majestic heights of understanding and goodwill. Therefore, I send an open letter to the unwise leader, his followers and non-followers:

Smoothen your rough edges

Dear unwise leader,
As a goldsmith sifts dust from gold;
Remo'e your impurities – hatred.
Conquer your thoughts;
Tame your words 'n master your actions.
Follow these paths with purity.

Dear followers of the unwise leader;
It matters not the many holy verses you have master'd.
The many divine tongues you speak.
Just be remind'd: ugly words hurt.
And, ugliness re-bounds.
Honour that hardly comes easy to your broad tongue – love!
For the pebbles we hold in our mouths destroy rather than build.

Dear non-followers of the unwise leader;
No enemy can harm you;
As much as your own thoughts, unguard'd.
Empathize with the unawaken'd;
And, your innate light will shine-out, effortlessly.
Smoothen your rough edges;
Subdue yourself, 'n disco'er your inner divinity.
Look at your faults not those of others.
For, dwellin' on your brother's imperfections only magnifies your own.

Awareness and commitment: first act against political violence

In this political quagmire, many Africans rightly ask: *I am only one; what can I do.* Answer: *Many things.* It all begins with the first step of awareness and commitment, which you have done by purchasing and reading this book.

To qualify the foregoing, I give a practical example. This happened back in 2004 in Kingston, Jamaica, during an international conference that I attended. As a last activity, the massive auditorium was intentionally plunged into pitch-darkness. A young lady stood at the centre holding a lit candle. She asked loudly: *I am only one; what can I do to change the status quo?* She then turned left and right lighting the candles of her two immediate neighbours. Then, the two moved to different parts of the auditorium; they repeated the question before lighting the candles of their two adjacent neighbours. This exercise was repeated until all candles in the auditorium were lit. The flame passed; the light spread; and, the room became a sea of light.

This confirms that you, as an individual, can do many things in the fight against political violence staining *the Fortress in a once Seemingly Peaceful Realm.* For, all personal and/or social change comes through simple acts repeated daily. A combination of those little bits of good deeds will eventually make *the Fortress* less frightening and a better place to live in. Thus,

Go forward 'n engage.
Find likeminded people;
Not from your social circle,
But anywhere in your community.
Change the opinions of hate-lovers;
Not with ridicule, but reason.

Throughout, keep in mind: as a citizen, you are the most important player in any political development in your community. For, Africa's power resides not in any fantasies of exceptionalism but in the souls of the ordinary people who risk their lives to re-imagine the contours of fairness, justice and citizenship – broadly defined. Moreover, the highest office in any country is the citizenry.

Oftentimes, the opponents of the status quo frequently point their fingers and say they cannot trust the proponents of the existent conditions; and, the vice versa. There is an old cliché, which fits here: when you point a finger at someone, there are three fingers pointing back to you. When you say, you do not trust those ruling, you are saying more about yourself than those you are opposing. Even worse, in the attempt to free yourself of the enemy without, you might be tempted to feed the enemy within. But then, to imitate the hatred and violence of tyrants and chauvinists is the best way to take their places. That is an option Africans must reject. Otherwise, the new order that you are fighting for will be nothing but a duplication of the old order.

Africans should resist all forms of cynicism and polarization, which would divide the continent into *us* versus *them*. Thence, all utterances and actions should reflect the decency of the African people. They should foster a sense of common purpose and usher a new beginning where Africa rise and fall as one. Thus, national/continental efforts must forever be geared towards restoring hope, maintaining commitments and promoting the well-being of all Africans. Citizens must move forward together, as one, in a renewed spirit of solidarity, cooperating generously – guided by the voice of love and fraternity; hope and fairness. For this is a voice that brings out the best in each of the members of a society.

For many in *the Fortress in a once Seemingly Peaceful Realm*, a future filled with countless possibilities beckons; yet many others remain disoriented and aimless, trapped in a hopeless maze of violence and despair. Their problems are your problems. You cannot assume them. Together, as a people, you must face them; talk about them; and, seek sustainable solutions jointly. For, no one can lead a happy life if he thinks only of himself and turns everything to serve his own interest. And, the yardstick you use for others will be the yardstick which time will use on you.

Consequently, if one wants security, he must give security; if one wants to be heard, he must listen; if one wants opportunities, he must provide opportunities. By so doing, Africans recognize a simple but powerful truth: they need each other. Ultimately, they nurture a culture-of-care, which directs them to constantly relate to each other. To reject a mind-set of hostility and instead adopt one of reciprocal subsidiarity, in a constant effort to do their best. To go forward therefore, is to march onward together. As you do so, let your goal be:

Where love's unknown;
Make it known.
Where fairness' elusive;
Make it nonelusive; and,
Where peace's impermanent;
Make it permanent.

Africans must be catalysed to work towards a future that is empathetic rather than polarized. They must care, vocally and actively, about the welfare of each other by embracing each other and being brave for each other. They need to be thoughtful in their actions. For any blind, angry protest is counter-productive and only strengthens those who do not share the national/continental pacific worldview. Passivity is not an option either.

Throughout the continent therefore, people must choose a middle ground based on active engagement. A genre of engagement that values the ideologies that differ from those of theirs. This enables one to creatively walk into the heart of the violent constituency and offer them real but passionate solutions instead of replicating their divisive narratives. Consequently, the intention should forever be to offer fellowship and unity rather than panning prejudice that stokes ethnic-related angers and hatreds as detailed in Chapter 2.

In brief, tangible changes in *the Fortress in a once Seemingly Peaceful Realm* will only be realized when those in positions of influence recognize that demonizing whole groups of people always backfires. Further, ordinary people have to appreciate the fact that they share more in common with each other than those in whose interest it is that they stay divided.

Concluding remarks

Genuine democracy rests on the unshakeable foundation of violence-free political process. Consequently, any form of intimidation results in deformed democracy. It is therefore, the onus of thinkers and writers to advocate for a saner and more inclusive view of Africa as a diverse community. A community in which everyone has as much to give as to receive; towards a common dream.

Common dream

With a common dream in sight.
Hold on to your persuasions.
With bitterness havin' no sway.
Make Africa the dream the original dreamers dreamt-of.
Where no man crushes another;
And, where fairness' the oxygen for all.

Build the continent together.
For, like islands in the sea,
You're separate on the surface;
But connect'd in the deep.
Tied together in a unifi'd garment of destiny.
For, whatever affects one directly affects all (in)directly.

Finally, it is of capital importance to note that, Africa's perfection will not result from the ascendancy of any excellence, but from the blending of what is best in each one of her citizen. Such a blending is stronger when people *rise by uplifting others*. This ushers us to the last phase, Part 2, of our safari *Beyond Negative Ethnicity, Corruption and Violence*.

PART 2

RISE BY UPLIFTING OTHERS

Rise by upliftin' others.
Train your mind to see the good in others.
Magnify their strengths, not their weaknesses.
For blowin'-out someone's candle;
Makes not yours brighter.

As the sun shines on the just 'n the unjust,
Shine your love equally to all.
For, your smile can uplift a soul.
Your word can frame a goal.
Your laugh can conquer gloom.
And, your love can make a difference.

Reject pessimism 'n embrace optimism.
Succumb not to cynicism in the face of darkness.
Light your candle 'n step forward.
Be true to yourself.
But, seek-out those who don't always agree with you.
That'll teach you the art-of-compromise.

To rise by upliftin' others;
You must understand yourself;
To understand others.
Allow light within you.
As the more light you allow in your heart,
The brighter your world'll be.
Throughout, ne'er let your successes go to your head;
And, ne'er let your failures go to your heart.
That'll usher you to the heart of *good leadership*.
Enablin' you to *extract the innate greatness of all*.

CHAPTER 8

Good Leadership: Extraction of Innate Greatness

True leader

He's a good leader.
A leader whose courage knows no end.
As he goes where there's no path;
And, leaves a trail.

He's a genuine leader.
A leader who elicits greatness in his followers.
As he inspires them to dream 'n learn;
To do more 'n become more.

He's a true leader.
A leader in whose followers, authentic love's reveal'd.
As he leads by example;
From behind.

Preamble

Leaders in Africa, like elsewhere, serve as the point of reference for their followers. They set the tone on issues related to negative ethnicity, corruption and violence. Consequently, leadership is the first of the four quintessential arsenals in the combat against the combined evils of *The hate-spewing Ruffians, The Blood-sucking Urchins* and *The Violence-spitting Vipers* presently ruining *the Fortress in a once Seemingly Peaceful Realm.*

In the context of this book, leadership is the capacity to lead people to their desired goals. Oftentimes, it also calls for the leader to help his followers shape those goals. For, in a goalless scenario, everyone is a flotsam and jetsam in an open sea with indeterminable destination. And, when a sailor knows not to which port he sails, no wind is favourable.

A true leader therefore, acts unselfishly and demands more from himself than from others. He defies adversity by doing what is right and moves beyond the common sense of the proponents of the status quo. He develops strategies to achieve set outcomes and modifies his approach(es) as necessary for he understands the importance of small actions consistently taken. He is not perfect, because perfection is not leadership; humanity is. This chapter takes this fact into consideration as it scrutinizes leadership as an antidote to negative ethnicity, corruption and violence in Africa.

Visionary and selfless African leaders

As postgraduate students in Europe, we regularly and passionately discussed personal strengths and deficiencies in African leaders. On the positive side we discussed visionary and selflessness - putting national interests ahead of personal gains. Under this category, we endlessly discussed Nelson Mandela,

Kwame Nkrumah (1909-72), Gamal Abdel Nasser (1918-70), Seretse Khama (1921-80), Julius Nyerere (1922-99), Samora Machel (1933-86), Boutros Boutros-Ghali (1922-2016), Kofi Annan (1938-2018), and Jerry Rawlings. In each case, we would conclude that these African sons embraced a leadership style that was founded on a solid ethical value system. A system hallmarked by inclusiveness, openness, fairness, and justice.

These leaders shared three common traits. Firstly, they were courageous and thus always did what was right and necessary rather than what was popular. As they understood that what is right is not always popular; and, what is popular is not always right. They had the ability to make hard decisions that were in their people's best interest.

Secondly, they had heightened levels of self-awareness. They were acutely aware of their personal strengths and limitations, which enabled them to exude a healthy sense of self-esteem – a quintessential element in ultimate leadership.

Thirdly, they were people-oriented and hence created more leaders rather than followers. Their legacies were therefore built not only on their personal successes, but also on the success of those they led.

Consequently, they were not great because of the power they wielded, but because of their ability to empower their followers. They were aware that their role as leaders was never to give greatness to others, but rather to help them extract the innate greatness in each of them. They appreciated the fact that, a mighty flame follows a tiny spark. Towards this end, they led by walking behind those they led.

Good leaders are servants of their followers

The world tends toward continuums. Linear continuity helps to capture and comprehend societal complexities. Leadership follows a similar continuum, one anchored by good and bad. In general, good leadership excites, energizes and stimulates. It shakes complacency and inertia into action. It ignites collective action and stirs passion.

Political leaders in *the Fortress in a once Seemingly Peaceful Realm* are important. This is so because they influence the distribution of resources and make decisions, which have far-reaching implications. For, in many cases, such decisions set the tone on how to deal with the triple monsters: negative ethnicity, corruption and violence - see for example Chapter 3. Hence, it is worth it to pay attention to the following qualities whenever selecting political representatives at all levels of governments.

A good (political) leader is an exemplar of integrity to the people he represents. Thus, he is honest and responsible for his actions and decisions. He rises by uplifting others as he builds bridges not walls; reconciles not alienates; and, unites not divides.

Importantly, a genuine leader has no attachment to any agenda as his beliefs are informed by those of his followers. Consequently, he is guided by goals that are specific, achievable and measurable with no unsustainable quick fixes. He recognizes that human spirit thrives best when goals are set and progress can be measured based on desired achievement. He thinks globally but acts locally as he recognizes that in order for the community to prosper, individuals must realize their dreams. This unleashes innate creative energy and intrinsic flair.

A true leader uses reliable and unfiltered information to make decisions, as he does not take what is similar to his views as fact. Otherwise, he becomes so secure in his bubble that he starts accepting only information, whether it is true or not, that fits his opinions, instead of basing them on the evidence that is tested.

He realises that self-delusion in the face of unpleasant facts is folly.

Above all, a good leader has a tamed ego. As used in this text, ego is a false-self, created by unconscious identification with one's mind. It is a derived sense-of-self as it identifies itself with external things like level of education, physical appearance, special abilities, family history, belief systems, political, racial, religions, and other collective identifications. Bloated ego with its attendant misgivings is the fountain of myriad forms of human shortcomings – chauvinism, deceit, greed, vanity, pomposity, hatred, licentiousness, malignancy, obstinacy and the list goes on – see the alphabet soup of vices enumerated in Chapter 2. Thus, pumped-up egos make us and our opinions seem better than others, and anyone else's wisdom, inferior.

Kibicho (2016: 99) puts it eloquently: *unrefined egos trick us to think that we are ascending, when in reality we are descending at a dizzying speed.* This is so because ego afflicts the soul: the worse the person is, the less he feels it; for it is similar to a sleeping person. Someone sleeping lightly perceives impressions in his dreams and is sometimes, even, aware during sleep that he is indeed sleeping. Conversely, a heavy slumber plunges the mind too deep for consciousness of self. This brings us to the question: why does an egoic person never admit his failings? Because he is deep in them; he is deep asleep. Only an awakened person recounts his dream, and acknowledging one's failings is a sign of awakeness. A more apt analogy would be that of a beer licking mouse.

Some alcohol spilt on the beer bar floor. When the pub's door closed for the night, a mouse crept out of his hole. He scanned the room for safety, and then comfortably sat on his haunches at the edge of the frothy foam. He leisurely lapped-up the foam until the floor was bone dry. Thereafter, he lay on his side. And, all night long, apart from spasmodic loud burps, he roared: *Bring on the goddamn fat cat!*

Similar to alcohol in the above story, wild ego begets a self-aggrandisement and an illusion, which overshadows our weaknesses and exaggerates our strengths. For a wild ego cannot distinguish what 'it knows' and what 'it does not know'. Consequently, to preserve its self-declared super status, the runaway ego transforms its bearer into a know-it-all being. Conversely, the antidote to egoism is wisdom. For, the more the wisdom, the lesser the ego; and, the less the wisdom, the more the ego. Thus, good leaders have tamed egos, which enables them to see through the eyes of their followers. They see with their ears and hear with their eyes. This brings us to a conversation I had recently with a martial arts Master in Okinawa, Japan.

> *This author:* Master, which crowd do you prefer… the one that adores and applauds you; or, the one that shouts insults at you…?
>
> *Master:* Neither, they all make noise… If you allow such noise to seep into your ego, it mutates into an internal monster that devours the best of you. It enslaves you to an image chasing after desire thereby creating inner turmoil.
>
> When egoism becomes the guide, chauvinists, fraudsters and gangsters are born. As a result, men fight against their souls and most lose everything in the face of egotism's massive destructive strength. It reduces giants into pygmies. For, it makes them think they are lions until it is time to do what lions do. Only when you know and accept that you are ordinary, will you be aware of human innate frailties and their power over you. Remain ego-free… [The Master advises].

Leadership as seen by Archbishop Desmond Tutu

Back in 2002, I had an informative discussion with Archbishop Desmond Tutu – another South African Apartheid icon. This discussion took place during an 11½hour flight from Amsterdam Schiphol Airport (the Netherlands) to Cape Town International Airport (South Africa), for I had the privilege of sitting next to Archbishop Tutu. We discussed many issues: religion, politics, climate change, the future of Africa and leadership. On the last topic, the renown Archbishop noted:

Good leadership is about protecting and advancing accepted principles through means to ends. There may be legitimate differences in interpretation of what is right and wrong; good and bad; but, the tried and time-tested values upon which every civilization is based are similar across culture and time. For, goodness heeds the best interests and welfare of others.

In many aspects, I equate a leader with a teacher. In this sense, the test of a good teacher is not how many questions he can ask his pupils that they will answer readily, but how many questions he inspires them to ask him, which he finds difficult to answer. Similarly, the task of leadership is not to put greatness into humanity, but to elicit it, for the greatness is already there. Thus, a good leader helps those who are doing poorly do well; and, those doing well to do even better. For, leadership is about unlocking people's potential.

Today's leadership is synonymous with ragged spirituality, divisions of all kinds, and emptiness in the lives of the followers. Thus, we find ourselves rich in goods, but ragged in spirit; we are torn by division, wanting unity; we see around us empty lives, wanting fulfilment. To find solutions, we need only to look within ourselves. When we listen to the better angels of our nature, we find that they celebrate the basic things such as love, kindness, fairness, and justice.

Consequently, good leadership should amplify these simple trappings. For, they are the most needed ingredients if we are to surmount what divides us, and cement what unites us. Once we realize this, we come to a deeper centre that shows us the foundations on which we must build, and the priorities we must seek. In fact, our anxiety about the future is a clear sign that we have placed our trust in the wrong places and in false things. Brief, people need leadership that will help them lift their eyes to the broad horizon ahead.

In sum therefore, there is no gainsaying the fact that the quest for leadership is an undeniable fact in human history, in all matters relating to the management of both human and material resources. Therefore, it is worth noting that the success of a society depends on the effectiveness of its leaders. For an army of sheep led by a lion can defeat an army of lions lead by a sheep. This makes me think of a good friend and colleague named Professor Skirt Chaser.

Professor Skirt Chaser was a dedicated land digger. He dug lands of all shapes and sizes. He did so with the help of his precariously ever-dangling digging hoe. A hoe appropriately named Mr. Dicks. Mr. Dicks' deep-penetrating mono-eye came in handy as it enabled the tag-team espy diggable lands from afar. And, together they loved land-digging in toto. Anon, the bald-headed Mr. Dicks took over Professor Skirt Chaser's thinking faculty. Thus, land-digging took a fresh meaning. Like noctambulists, they furiously dug and re-dug; both virgin and explored lands; with or without permission from the landowners. For, they thoroughly enjoyed the art of land-digging.

Result: Professor Skirt Chaser got more than he bargained for. He died of HIV/AIDS-related complications. Brief, massive investment towards the attainment of professorship, pinnacle of academic totem pole, and a promising land-digging career were all for naught due to Mr. Dicks' mediocre and short-sighted leadership. A prime example of a sheep leading a lion.

Concluding remarks

Before I conclude this Chapter, let me share one of my favourite lessons from my esteemed teacher Seneca. He told me: *misdeeds are greatly diminished if a witness is always standing near intending doers.* Consequently, I suggest that each of us set our affection on some good man and keep him constantly before our eyes. Thus, we live as if he were watching over us. He becomes the standard against which our characters can measure themselves. For, without a ruler to do it against, you would not make the crooked straight. Thus, choose someone whose way of life and whose very face as mirroring the character that lies behind it, have won your approval. If you like therefore, attach yourself to Plato and Miyamoto Musashi: the first one will give a knowledge of man and universe, the other how to steel your spirit and brace it against whatever threatens. Moreover, a person who is able to revere another, will soon deserve to be revered himself.

Back to leadership in *the Fortress in a once Seemingly Peaceful Realm*... In the Africa's set up, political leadership is at the heart of expanding rings of interconnected social networks that link leaders directly and/or indirectly with the citizens. These linkages may be physical and/or psychical. Subsequently, the choices the leaders make or fail to make affect everything and everyone for they sit at the apex of societal expectations' totem pole.

For the benefit of all therefore, a leadership creativity that combines ideas and action(s) is long overdue in *the Fortress*. This kind of innovativeness produces conditions that are different from the existing ones that are hallmarked by stinking negative ethnicity, faceless corruption and senseless violence. The driver of such a leadership is as authentic as a lighthouse.

The lighthouse

An authentic leader's a lighthouse.
As he guides ships through the turbulent darkness.
He lights the right path for his followers.
Moti'ates them to dream 'n reach.
To know, to grow 'n to glow.
Molds his followers into precious gems.
By helpin' them walk upon the unwalk'd.
For, he sees potential 'n believes in the best in others.

He talks with crowds 'n keeps his virtue;
Walks with kings 'n ne'er loses his common touch.
Dreams without makin' dreams his master.
Waits without getting' tir'd of waitin'.
Be lied about without dwellin' in lies.
Be hated without givin' way to hatin'.
For, he's love:
The mother of all virtues.

CHAPTER 9

Love: The Mother of All Virtues

Love not hate

Africa needs to revert to her core-values.
And, unleash the creati'ity 'n potential of all.
Africans need not to always agree on all issues.
But, they need to believe in their mutual responsibility.
For, human identity depends on the passin' of ideals to the next generation.

Throughout, justice must be the shield 'n defender.
For, justice is not a political menu option;
But, rather a definin' commitment of the continent.
'Tis the wave of her future.
As, desire for justice's not confined to, or own'd by a few;
'Tis an innate hope of all.
Thence, justice'll not be serv'd till those who're unaffect'd are as outrag'd as those who are.
...Till, the strong are just 'n the weak are valu'd.

Love not hate.
Only love'll save Africa from the forces tearin' her apart.
For, hatred doesn't cease by hatred; but only by love.
Be a voice for compassion 'n a silencer to indifference.
Be not indifferent to the hatred you see, hear 'n feel.
For, the hatred you see;
Can't survive a lovin' view.
The hatred you hear;
Can't make it through the voice of compassion.
The hatred you feel;
Can't live long when forgiveness takes action.

Preamble

Love is the second armament in the fight against *The hate-spewing Ruffians, The Blood-sucking Urchins* and *The Violence-spitting Vipers* currently ruling *the Fortress in a once Seemingly Peaceful Realm*. Authentic love would give Africans the courage to unite, regardless of their differences. It will enable them see each other as brothers and sisters; and, thus value the unescapable garment of destiny that unite them as allies in human spirit. This is the ultimate remedy to negative ethnicity, corruption and violence as practised in Africa.

The genre of love espoused in this Chapter spreads through a lock-step synchronization of countenance, body movement, language, and attitudes. It is hallmarked by a smile, a hug, a kind word and a show of empathy, all of which have universal meaning(s). For, they activate similar empathetic responses irrespective of one's physical appearance.

Love is the mother of other virtues: tolerance, fairness, justice to name but a few. Once these values inform Africans priorities and reactions, they will be able to see themselves in each other. This will safeguard dignity for all, especially the most vulnerable in *the Fortress in a once Seemingly Peaceful Realm*. Subsequently, all lives will be enriched and humanity shines. For, as noted elsewhere, the greatness of a society is reflected by how it treats its less fortunate.

The art of loving our antagonists

Over 2000 years ago, there was a humorous but serious man who loved to walk in the towns of Canaan, Galilee, Jericho, Jerusalem, Judea and other neighbouring ancient centres. According to his many friends, he did weird things. He walked on water; turned fishermen into fishers-of-men; dined with a woman of loose morals; fed a multitude of over 5,000 with five barley loaves and two tiny fishes; and, transformed water into beer. [I guess many followers adored him for his ability to perform the last one]. In addition, he used an idiosyncratic language that many people still find difficult to decipher. He once said: *Love your neighbour as yourself.*

Once we grow in love, we are able to love ourselves. I tell a personal story to explain how this works. For my Doctorate training, I had to be near excellent in the language of delivery – French. Consequently, I enrolled in a Summer University in Lyon, France, for an intensive three months French programme. And, French language can be very complicated especially to students like me who have difficulties mastering even their mother tongues. You need to have a language mind - a real knowledge of how to use the two principal verbs of *etrê* (to be) and *avoir* (to have). You have to literally memorize how to conjugate over a hundred verbs in several ways – past, present, future, conditional, subjective and their varying derivatives.

Céline was a close friend and a fellow classmate who could do her French homework in about an hour while it took me over two hours. The more I tried to do it like her, the more frustrated I became. I was unwilling to accept my limitations. Eventually, I had to come to a very hard conclusion, and tell myself: *Wanjohi Kibicho, Céline Marque is better in French than you. She can finish in an hour what takes you two to three hours.* With that recognition, I accepted myself with all my limitations. I loved myself.

Nonetheless, the kind of love the aforementioned peculiar man from Jerusalem had in mind goes beyond loving oneself. A type of love that causes one to love the person who does the evil deed while hating the deed he committed – love the sinner, but hate the sin. This takes us back to my Doctorate training.

As a prerequisite, I had to take a certain statistics-related course. Within ten minutes into our first class, the course Professor paused and emphatically informed me in an arrogant, condescending and demeaning manner that I was in the wrong class. I responded respectfully, *I am in the right class, Sir.* This incensed him to the extreme. In front of my classmates, he angrily continued: *Poor 'man of colour', you have absolutely no chance of succeeding in this Course.* Reflexively, I took my weathered notebook from the pocket, the one with my *Life Lesson*, and quickly scanned through the front page: *Have no moral middle ground and refuse indifference as an option to violence. Be unyielding and inflexible in its opposition. Be intelligent...* Calmly, I deeply breathed-in and out. Maintaining direct eye contact with the instructor, I firmly said: *Thank you very much Professor for letting me know early in the Semester that my possibility of passing your Course is nil. Nonetheless, deep in me, there is a strong voice telling me that, I am going to do pretty well in this Course.* This tense exchange continued for a while until the teacher lost it. He dismissed the class.

Before anyone left the class, I loudly and clearly observed: *If I have said anything that overstates the truth and indicates disrespect, I beg your forgiveness. If I have said anything that understates the truth and reflects respect that allows me to settle for anything less than fair treatment, I beg forgiveness from the celestial sphere.* The entire class exploded in my support. They gave me a round of applause, which further enraged the Professor. He quickly walked out of the classroom mumbling incoherently. I had a mixed feeling: I looked for the best and I was ready for the opposite.

In the first written test, I scored 81 percent, the highest marks in the class while the second best student scored 63 percent. I completed this Course at the top of the class with a weighted mean score of 87 percent.

Six years after the fore-described anomalous verbal exchange, the Professor in question was nominated to the European Union Parliament. He invited me to his office in Brussels, Belgium, for 'a cup of coffee' – his words not mine. During that meeting, he told me: *It has always been my feeling that something I said in class six years back annoyed you.* I smiled then a tirade of words broke free: *No, you did not. For, no man annoys me. I have absolute no ill will for anyone, but I have an abhorrence for hatred, bigotry and demagoguery.* He continuously interjected in an attempt to exonerate his past behaviour. At the end, I politely made it clear to him that I love him as a person but I hated, and still hate, what he did to me in front of my colleagues in our first class. By so doing:

I unburden'd a heavy heart;
He apologis'd profusely;
We remain in contact.
And, that's the power of love.

We can only achieve the foregoing when we move beyond *loving* to *being love* – as instructed by President Mandela (see *Prologue*). To *be love* however, we must be receptive to love; possess love; comprehend love; be vulnerable to love; and, grow in love.

Be love

To recognize love;
You must be recepti'e to love.
For, you can't appreciate what you don't recognize.
To give love;
You must possess love.
For, you can't give what you don't possess.

To teach love;
You must comprehend love.
For, you can't teach what you don't understand.
To yield to love;
You must be vulnerable to love.
For, you can't admit what you don't yield to.

To dedicate yourself to love;
You must grow in love.
For, you can't love what you don't dedicate yourself to.

Love unifies the human family

A candle can light thousands of candles without losing its flame or its life being shortened – see the candle lighting exercise in Kingston, Jamaica detailed in Chapter 7. Likewise, love never diminishes for being shared. Nonetheless, if you expect others to make you loving or loveable, you have missed the boat. For genuine love is like breaking an egg. If an external force breaks it, life ends. Contrastingly, if an internal force breaks it, life begins. Similarly, love that sees no limits springs from within and never from without. It should be centred within you. As my revered teachers taught me: *It comes from within...* (see *Acknowledgment Section*). That said, the basis for loving others is the love that you have for yourself: *Love thy neighbour as thyself.*

With that,

> *I welcome you to 'The Perspective-Changing Club';*
> *'The Club of Love'.*
> *For you have now paid,*
> *Your lifetime membership dues.*

The earlier mentioned man from Jerusalem envisaged a kind of love that equips us with a unique pair of lenses that enables us to see beyond skin pigments; style of belief; preference of sexual partner; and, gender identity. Instead, we see the crimson of blood, the beating of the heart and the unique manifestation of divinity. Eventually, we only value the common threads and the unescapable garment of destiny that unite us as allies in one big human family. For we are all the same at our core, connected in human spirit. The courage to unite, regardless of differences, is what will truly make *the Fortress in a once Seemingly Peaceful Realm* beautiful and unique.

Once we dedicate ourselves to this kind of love, humility sets-in with all its glorious trappings for it opens more doors than arrogance. Just like a baker bakes, a plumber unblocks pipes and a writer writes; arrogance repels, humility inspires and wisdom illuminates. Thus, ensure you are inspiring and illuminating by being humble and wise.

Remain humble and wise

Be humble.
A humble person makes room for progress;
A proud person believes he's already there.
Remain humble!

Plato, my teacher, once told me:
I am strong, because I've been weak.
I am fearless, because I've been afraid.
I am wise, because I've been foolish.
Remain wise!

Plato is creatively and gently reminding us that to be old and wise, one must be young and stupid first. As it takes sadness to know what happiness entails; noise to appreciate silence; and, absence to value presence. Once this appreciation sets in, humility solidifies. Such humility and a dose of wisdom help us to add value to lives of those around us; see the good in others, and then treat them as if that is all we see. It enables us to place virtue before vice; values before vanity; and, principles before personalities. Eventually, we end up respecting even those who do not deserve to be respected; not as a reflection of their character, but a true reflection of our inner-self.

Be your neighbours' keeper

As the overarching theme of this Chapter is love, I dare say: let us love each other without condition; and, talk with each other with no ill intentions. Let us support each other without reason; and, care for one another with no expectations. For this is the greatest expression of love. A kind of love that replaces evil with good; meanness with generosity; and, lies with truth. This genre of love calls us to be our neighbour's keeper. For, no man can be fully free if his neighbour is not. Let me dramatize this a bit through story telling.

One evening, Mr. *Panya* the mouse peeped from his hiding spot under the old tattered sofa. He saw the farmer and his wife enthusiastically open unusual looking package. *It must be cheese*, he convinced himself. Quickly his mouth-watering juvenile imagination turned into a nightmare on realisation that it was a state of the art mousetrap. He decided to go to the barnyard and share the bad news with his long-time friends.

He approached the family cockerel and melodramatically broke the sad news: *There is a mousetrap in the house!* [He repeated the message several times while aimlessly running in circles.] *Please come with me. We need to go and dismantle that trap.* The cockerel clucked and scratched, raised his majestic head and lordly retorted: *Mr. Panya, I know this new trap must be a concern to you, but it is of no consequence to me. It bothers me not. Get out of my bedroom, I want to sleep!* The terror-stricken mouse approached Milly the she-goat, and repeated the same message. Showing no sympathy, Milly castigated her friend for worrying over a small matter. She said: *A mousetrap cannot be a goat's problem. You should learn to graciously carry your own cross. If I were you, I would simply keep-off the farmer's house!* She arrogantly advised the petrified mouse before retiring to bed.

Dejected, *Mr. Panya* returned to the main house to deal with the mousetrap alone. At about midnight, a bang noise echoed throughout the house. It was a sound of a mousetrap catching its prey. The disturbance woke the farmer up. He excitedly hurried to the dining room to celebrate the demise of the annoying mouse. In darkness, he did not see it was a black mamba, the most venomous land snake in Africa, whose tail was caught in the trap. The snake bit the farmer!

The wife took the farmer to the nearby health centre, and he returned home with fever. As wisdom dictates, the wife decided to treat the fever with fresh chicken soup. So, the cockerel became the soup's main ingredient. Nevertheless, her husband's illness persisted which brought in relatives, friends and neighbours. To feed them, the farmer's wife slaughtered Milly the she-goat. Mr. *Panya* lived lonely in the farmyard thereafter.

Brief, next time you hear your neighbour has a problem, listen to him and keep an eye out for him, for we are all together in this journey of life. That should be your spirit; the African spirit; and, the spirit of humanity. For, in the absence of love, we end up with solutions that do not solve; answers that do not answer; and, explanations that do not explain.

Unlearn to hate

No one is born hating others because of their bodily characteristics – see also Chapter 2. None of us was aware of such superficial descriptions at birth. In fact, experts on child development show that acquisition of positive and/or negative attitudes towards other people begins at the pre-school age. Thus, it is fair to argue that as we learn more about ourselves, we also learn to love those who look and behave like us. Learning to hate takes a similar process.

Thence, the procedure of countering hatred with love should start at an early stage. With proper training, nothing is beyond reach. It turns bad morals to good, kills bad principles and generates good ones. It can lift ethnic chauvinists to angelhood; turn corrupt individuals into saints; and, transform violent beings to deities. Towards this end, the power of reinforcement should be the organizing principle of such training.

This principle is premised on the theory that any pattern of behaviour that is consistently reinforced becomes an automatic and conditioned response. Inversely, anything that lacks reinforcement dissipates. Positive reinforcement takes place when we give a reward each time the desired behaviour is exhibited. That reward can be a simple praise and/or a gift. This must follow immediately after the behaviour takes place, as appropriate timing is critical to effective conditioning. For instance, when a mother tells her eleven-year old son, *I am proud of you son,* immediately after he defends a mentally-unwell man, it has a more lasting impact than if she waited until the boy turned twenty years old – see Chapter 5. Why? Because, the learner must connect the sensations of reinforcement with the behavioural pattern that is taking place. This is in line with Ivan Pavlov's dog conditioning. This is referred to as the *Theory of Classical Conditioning*. I give you an example to make it less frightening.

To train a dolphin to jump, trainers wait for the animal to jump on its own, then reward it with a fish. By so doing each time the dolphin jumps, the mammal makes the link between jumping and getting a fish. In this scenario, 'jumping' is the behaviour the trainer wants while 'getting the fish' is the pleasure the dolphin seeks. Pairing of pleasure to a required behaviour allows the trainer to condition the dolphin to jump. Upon learning the behaviour, the trainer changes the tactic: He gives fish only when the dolphin jumps higher. For, if the dolphin is rewarded after every jump, it becomes habituated and will no longer give its full effort. To deal with possible slacking therefore, the trainer rewards the dolphin sometimes after the first jump or perhaps after the fifth. The animal is never sure which jump will be rewarded. This sense of anticipation that a reward may be given, coupled with the uncertainty as to which try will be rewarded, causes the dolphin to consistently give its hundred percent. This ensures that the reward is never taken for granted.

The same strategy can be used to cultivate a long-lasting behaviour in human beings. Nevertheless, it is invaluable that the trainer understands and utilizes a clear schedule of reinforcement. As we reinforce good behaviour, we need to keep in mind that talking about differences does not boost prejudice –

see chapters 2 and 3. For, awareness does not lead to negative attitudes.

Nevertheless, while we want our children to understand things that bind us as human beings, it is essential they also understand that shared characteristics and other cultural traits are expressed in different ways. Having said that, parents must give their children accurate information and guide them when their behaviours evince sparks of hatred. Above all, parents should ensure their words of wisdom are in tune with their actions. For, children are great imitators. They should be given something worthwhile to imitate.

Concluding remarks

Our beliefs do not make us better persons; our actions do. Similarly, good deeds are not done by walking into places of worship. They are done when we walk out of those places and help others; when we rise by uplifting others. They are realized when we walk-the-talk as preaching with our lives rather than with our lips is a superior sermon. And, to give pleasure to a single necessitous soul by a single act of love is more powerful than a thousand of heads bowing in prayer.

Leading from the above therefore, one cannot gainsay the fact that blowing your neighbour's candle out does not make yours any brighter. Hence, as the sun shines equally on the poor and the rich; on the sinner and the saint, manifest your love and kindness for the benefit of all in *the Fortress in a once Seemingly Peaceful Realm*. As you do so, always take *failure as a stepping-stone to success;* and, *as a rung on the ladder* towards the promised land of good life.

CHAPTER 10

Failure: A Stepping Stone to Success

A rung on the ladder

Failure filters out what endures.
It strips away theinessential.
Permittin' us to learn from the past;
Givin' an opportunity to wisely begin again.

Failure's the sure-fire steppin' stone to success.
'Tis a learnin' experience;
A rung on the ladder; and,
A plateau at which we prepare to wisely try again.
For, when we're not failin',
We're growin' not.

Preamble

Accepting failure at all levels – personal, family, community, national and continental –, is the third essential strategy for dealing with *The Hate-spewing Ruffians, The Blood-sucking Urchins* and *The Violence-spitting Vipers*. Otherwise, citizens become doubtful of themselves followed by anxiety with all its crippling siblings. This energizes the angels of negative ethnicity; invigorates the goddesses of corruption; and, electrifies the deities of violence. Conversely therefore, both Africans and Africa herself should regard failure as the sure-fire stepping stone to success in this must-win battle.

Oftentimes, human beings falter under pressure. Pilots crash while divers drown; martial artists cannot perform a *kata*; basket-ballers fail to find the basket; and, golfers cannot find the pin. Their game plan collapses mid-way as they over-think the possibility of failing. They eye the prize instead of the act at hand; focus on the destination instead of the journey, which compromise their otherwise mastered fluidity – see also Chapter 1. Thus, they are different players – playing with the slow, cautious deliberations of a beginner. And, in a sense, they are beginners again!

Learning from experience is central to an individual's as well as a society's adaptation and survival. In more specific terms, failure in human life stimulates the search for new and more creative approaches. This should be the point of departure as *the Fortress in a Seemingly Peaceful Realm* battles with the triple fearsome giants: *The Hate-spewing Ruffians, The Blood-sucking Urchins* and *The Violence-spitting Vipers*.

Challenges refine your inner-self

Challenges are normal in life. How you view them defines you. If you choose to see them as stepping stones, then they become learning opportunities – see for example Chapter 4. They generate positive energy with its attendant invigorating effects. You develop an empowering mind-set that tells you:

I can!
We can!
Africa can!
Humanity can!

You should not be afraid of your weaknesses or inadequacies, for there is greatness in each of us. When you lack confidence in yourself, you become anxious and doubt your ability. Do not doubt yourself. Prepare well; and, once you have done that, be calm and confident. For, it is only with a peaceful mind that you can be efficient in your actions. In a peaceful mind, you enjoy adequate perception of the world as only in quiet waters things mirror themselves undistorted. In this state, you see things as they are supposed to be. A popular wheelbarrow story is worth re-telling to drive this point home. The story goes...

Every other Friday a security guard at *the Wheelbarrow Factory* saw a worker coming out of the factory pushing a wheelbarrow full of dirt. The guard searched inside the dirt, found nothing and let the worker go. This ritual repeated over several years until a time when the guard was about to retire from *the Wheelbarrow Factory*. When the man pushing the wheelbarrow appeared at the gate, he told him: *I know you are stealing something. I am just about to retire and this is my last day here. I will not tell anybody, but, please, tell me what you have been stealing from the Wheelbarrow Factory!* The man smiled and answered, *oh, I am not stealing dirt... I am stealing wheelbarrows!*

Brief, avoid all forms of distractions, both internal and external, that would otherwise muddle your faculties. That is the only way you will be able to see that the man pushing the wheelbarrow is actually *stealing a wheelbarrow.*

Take a break from whatever you are doing if necessary; go for a walk; and, spend a little time with your loved ones. But, do not get distracted by unproductive undertakings like negative ethnicity and all forms of violence. Take full control over your life, but remain hopeful if things do not work out as planned. Doing your very best might not take you to your preferred destination, but it will ultimately give you personal contentment.

Take every failure as a stepping-stone to success for each failure teaches us something. In any case, no matter how prepared you are, there is one thing that is guarantee: once you are on the river of life, you are definitely going to hit a few rocks. That is not pessimism but rather being realistic. The key is that when you run aground, instead of beating yourself up for failing, learn from the experience - pick yourself up and dust yourself off. For, the only safe harbour in our modern troubled sea of life is not to be bothered about what the future will bring and to stand steady and confident; and, to take without skulking or flinching whatever fortune throws at you. A recount of Soichiro Honda's (1906-91) life story is timely.

In 1938, while he was still in school, Mr. Honda started a small workshop in his family backyard. From here, he developed the concept of a piston ring with an intention of selling the product to Toyota Corporation. His first piston rings did not meet the Corporation's strict standards. Consequently, he had to go back to school for two more years. Throughout, his instructors and fellow students joked about the absurdity of his designs. Mr. Honda continued undistracted.

Upon graduation, Toyota gave him another contract, but he encountered another problem. The Japanese government was gearing up for World War II (1939-45), and therefore could not give him the concrete that he needed to construct his factory. As a result, Mr. Honda and his small team invented a process to make their own concrete with which they built the factory. The plant was bombed twice during *the War* thereby hindering his ability to meet Toyota's rising demand for piston rings. Finally, an earthquake destroyed the factory leaving Mr. Honda with no option but to sell his piston operation to Toyota.

After *the War*, a tremendous gasoline shortage hit Japan. Mr. Honda could not afford gas for his car. In desperation, he attached a small motor to his bicycle. On seeing this, his neighbours asked him to make 'motorized bikes' for them. Quickly his stock of motors ran-out. He decided to build a plant to manufacture motors to meet the new demand, but he did not have the start-up capital. He appealed to bicycle shop owners in mainland Japan who advanced the required capital. Eventually, he developed a lighter, scaled-down version of his motorbike. It was an instant success, which earned him the *Order of the Sacred Treasure (First Class)*, the highest honour bestowed by Japan's Emperor. Later, he exported his motorbikes to Europe and the USA, following up with the Honda cars that we know today. Presently, the Honda Corporation is one of the biggest car-making empires in the world.

Clearly, Mr. Honda had a strong resolve to succeed; he modified his approach accordingly until he produced the required results. The story reminds us that, when our action does not produce the desired result, we have not failed. We have only found a way that would not work. It teaches us that success is not an overnight experience. It results from making small decisions along the way: following up; taking action; persisting; and, retaining our focus on the task. Throughout, we need to hold ourselves to a higher standard and to learn from experience. Thus, the defeat of *the Lance-launching Cavalry* by *The Hate-spewing Ruffians*; the slaughter of *the Arch-shooting Squadron* by *The Blood-sucking Urchins*; and, the vanquishment of *the Waterball-slinging Platoon* by *The Violence-spitting Vipers* in *the Fortress in a once Seemingly Peaceful Realm* is due to the failure by *the War Council* to embrace this simple but unshakeable truth.

Otherwise put, the challenge that Africa faces with regards to negative ethnicity, corruption and violence is the result of not thinking of the potential consequences of individual and collective actions. Africans are so focused on selfish instantaneous gratification that their short-term solutions often become long-term problems. Like sleepwalkers therefore, many citizens continue with their unrelenting pursuit of quick fixes: video games, alcohol and drug abuse, fast food, instant pudding and microwave brownies. Similarly, youngsters throughout *the Fortress in a once Seemingly Peaceful Realm* hardly pay attention in school partly because they are addicted to this unsustainable immediate satisfaction. Living in this contorted sense of right and wrong, they fumble, ignorant of life's dynamics, expecting abundant rewards for nothing. Totally swamped by the mirage of luxury and consumerism; and, oblivious of their debilitating effects, they desire the entire world as well as heaven free of charge. A clear proof that mind-blindness is the worst form of handicap.

Courtesy of this mind-blindness, *the Fortress* is breeding a generation of invalids who cannot drink water from a glass unassisted. They wish for and pursue the impossible without realizing the inherent futility. Ultimately, their lives become battlegrounds of contradictions with ill-rounded jealousies and false alarms. As parental extravagance and weak values are the only form of education that they are given. For, parents protect them from the reality of life, packing them into capsules and then leaving them to effortlessly float in a false world. A true disaster waiting to explode.

The path to great things passes through failure

Stars cannot shine without darkness and diamonds cannot be polished without friction. Similarly, a man cannot be perfected without trials. Logically therefore, our trials, temptations and disappointments strengthen the fibre of our character. For, every endured trial ennobles our souls; every conquered temptation invigorates our moral energy; and, every weathered disappointment bolsters our resolve.

For reiteration-sake therefore, failure is inevitable in life. In fact, living a failure-free life is ceasing to live – in which case, you fail by default. Failure teaches you things about yourself that you could have learnt no other way. It makes you better, stronger and wiser. How so? Certainly, people of goodwill will be there to help you; to teach you; to guide you along your path. But, the lesson to be learnt remains yours. Of signal importance though, do not muddy the journey by avoiding its twists and bumps – see also Chapter 4. Rather embrace its life lessons, and strive to be and do better. Throughout, remain determined and hopeful. For, nothing is impossible to a determined and hopeful soul. When life knocks you down; pick yourself up; dust yourself off; and, start all over again. Do not lose hope when you slip, instead pick yourself up again and again. This is the only way you will make tangible and positive change in your life, in your society and in *the Fortress in a Seemingly Peaceful Realm* at large.

I repeat, progress in life is about baby steps. Just because you took longer than others to reach the mountain summit, does not mean you are a failure or weak. Even Albert Einstein (1879-1955) was expelled from high school several times for his below par performance, poor attitude and the negative effect that he had on his peers. It took him relatively longer to complete his high school education. While Einstein remained unknown in his earlier lives, he became one of the greatest scientific minds that ever lived. His *Theory of General Relativity*[1] revolutionized the scientific world. At his prime, everyone wanted a piece of him – Americans, French and Germans claimed Einstein to be one of their own. A reconfirmation of the dictum: Cry and you cry alone; smile and the world smiles with you. Keep smiling dear reader.

When you get undesired results, when plans go awry and the landscape suddenly changes, rather than becoming hopeless, pause and get back to the drawing board. Design new plans, form new alliances and discover new opportunities. Remain calm, smart and strategic. Nevertheless, as you pursue your dreams, you may often hear the words: *It will never happen or it is*

---

[1]Through the *Theory of General Relativity*, Albert Einstein proved that the laws of physics are the same for all non-accelerating observers. He showed that the speed of light within a vacuum is the same no matter the speed at which an observer travels. As a result, he found that space and time were interwoven into a single space-time continuum. Events that occur at some time for one observer could occur at different times for another.

very difficult. These voices will come from others and even from deep within yourself. Do not believe them. Instead, reach for the heavens and keep pushing forward and learn everything you can along the way. You will learn more from a glorious failure than you ever will from uncompleted tasks. Nonetheless,

There might be stress.
You may be in distress.
But, don't let pressure get hold of you.
Keep your hope alive;
Stand strong with focus 'n calmness;
Take care of yourself 'n believe in self.

At the end, none of your effort will go in vain. Your pain will be rewarded and your hard work will bring you unparalleled gain. But then, be reminded: the highest reward for man's toil is not what he gets for it, but what he becomes by it. Thus, be yourself, express yourself and have faith in yourself. Do not go out and look for a successful personality and duplicate it. Be the first rate version of yourself. In the process, however,

> *Weepin' may come at midnight;*
> *But, rejoicin' comes in the morning.*
> *For, resurrection follows crucifixion.*
> *So, keep your eyes beyond the prize.*

I summarize this *Section* by reiterating the fact that failing is an important part of the journey of life. Looking like a fool sometimes is the only way forward. Stay positive, and make your best efforts in whatever you do. Worry less. Life has taught me that worrying worsens whatever situation we are in. Take the time to celebrate all that you have accomplished so far in this precious journey of life. Crucially, own it and be proud of it. Therefore, you should:

- Believe you can; and, you will be halfway there;
- Do the common things uncommonly well;
- Strive for excellence, not perfection; and,
- Step forward. If you do not, you will forever remain where/what you are. You have to start, for you need not to be great to start, but you have to start to be great.

In an equal measure, never:

- Let what you cannot do interfere with what you can do;
- Wish it were easier; instead, wish you were better;
- Regret what you have done; rather, regret what you never did when you had the opportunity; and,
- Let your victories go to your head, or your failures go to your heart.

Concluding remarks

Never be ashamed of yourself for failure to realize your goals. You should compare such a failure with a clouds that drift in front of the sun without ever defeating its light. Thus, be proud of who you are, and do not worry about how others see you. For, you will never be good enough for everybody, but you will always be the best for someone who really cares for you. In any case, your value does not decrease based on someone's inability to see your worth.

The inherent law of mind states that we increase whatever we praise. Thus, we promote abilities by highlighting our achievements. For a more profound engagement with life-related complexities, you must be gentle with yourself first in order to be gentle with others. You must love yourself first before you love others. Towards this end therefore, your first step is to find the good and praise it; to give without remembering and receive without forgetting; and ultimately *being grateful of who you are*.

CHAPTER 11

Be Grateful of Who You Are

Goodness in everything

Gratefulness' the gateway to happiness.
It helps you rejoice for what you have;
Instead of grievin' for what you've not.
Helps you take pride of your excellences.
Makin' you relish them;
Both freshly 'n naively.

Find goodness in everythin',
And, a blade-of-grass becomes indescribably magnificent.
That's the power of gratitude;
That spurs you on to prove yourself worthy,
Of what others have done for you.
That's the essence of gratitude;
Which nurtures human soul.
Your soul!

Preamble

As used in this book, gratitude is a deeper appreciation for someone and/or something whether tangible or intangible, which produces longer lasting positivity. It enables people to acknowledge the goodness in their lives and to connect to worldly and transcendent elements - other beings, nature, and higher power. Thus, one says yes to life acknowledging both intrinsic and extrinsic goodness in all.

Moreover, scientific studies reveal that grateful individuals enjoy a saner body-mind-soul connection. They are more optimistic, more agreeable, more open, and less neurotic than those who are not (Wood et al., 2008). Further, they have more energy, more social connections and more satisfied with life. Thus, they are less likely to be depressed, envious, greedy or egoic.

Related to the above therefore, the inherent 'contagious nature of gratitude'[2] makes it a formidable fourth tool in battling the unified dark forces of *The Hate-spewing Ruffians, The Blood-sucking Urchins* and *The Violence-spitting Vipers* currently staining the image of *the Fortress in a once Seemingly Peaceful Realm*. Thus, gratefulness will enable Africans appreciate all that makes Africa what she is.

Authentic imperfections are the true beauty of humanity

Be thankful of what you have and who you are. For, when you concentrate on what you do not have, you will never have enough. The following fictitious dialogue eloquently captures the foregoing.

---

[2]*The Theory of Reciprocity* posits that when someone performs an act of gratitude for another person, that person will be motivated to do something gracious for the former person, or extend it to a stranger.

Ms. *Kunguru* the crow lived deep in Shimba Hills National Reserve. She was happy with her life. But one day, she saw Ms. *Njiwa* the dove. *Oh my goodness, she is so beautiful. By comparison, I am dark and dull,* she thought. She approached *Njiwa* and a conversation ensued:

Kunguru: You are so beautiful. You must be the happiest bird alive.

Njiwa: I used to think so, but then I saw Ms. *Kasuku* the parrot. Her chest is so red and vibrant. I feel so plain by comparison. I think Ms. *Kasuku* is the happiest bird alive.

[A few days later, *Kunguru* visited *Kasuku* at her home at the east-end of the Reserve].

Kunguru: Hello madam *Kasuku*. You are so beautiful. You must be the happiest bird alive.

Kasuku: I thought the same, until I saw Ms. *Tausi* the peacock. Her colours are rich and impressive. My chest looks so boring by comparison. I think Ms. *Tausi* is the happiest bird alive.

[A fortnight later, *Kunguru* paid *Tausi* a visit at her office at the main entrance of the Reserve. Many people flocked to *Tausi's* cage and took photographs. When the crowd left, *Kunguru* approached *Tausi*].

Kunguru: You are so beautiful. You must be the happiest bird alive.

Tausi: [*With a sigh*] I thought I was the happiest bird alive; then human beings put me in this tiny cage because of my beauty. Oftentimes, I look to the sky and see *Kunguru* flying free, and all I want is to be a *Kunguru*. I think you are the luckiest bird alive.

The gist of this story is that by comparing yourself to others, you lose sight of your own strengths. This is anathema to the secret to happiness which is to be thankful for what you have rather than concentrating on what you do not have. It is based on the fact that, the beginning of a habit is like an invisible thread. Every time you repeat an act you strengthen the strand. It gets stronger each time you add new filaments to it, eventually becoming a formidable cable that binds humanity irrevocably. Make your invisible thread a positive one and appreciate it. Because, with the virtue of gratitude, the wasteland of lack disintegrates and the entire *Fortress in a once Seemingly Peaceful Realm* experiences heaven on earth. So, measure your worth based on who you are and not what you have.

Undoubtedly, some people are going to dislike you, not because of something that you have done (to them), but because of various jealous reactions and other self-serving reactions that are inherent in the very human nature – see chapters 2 and 11. When such people treat you poorly for no reason, do not try to win their approval. At the same time, leave no space in your heart to hate them. Just walk away because the time you spend on such characters will be wasted, and any hatred in your heart will only hurt you. This is so because, hatred by nature destroys the very structure of the personality of the hater. For,

> *Hatred has no power to create.*
> *It distorts 'n defiles;*
> *Steals beauty 'n disrupts harmony.*
> *It silences the truth 'n ridicules virtue.*

Similarly, have no room for anger. As unrestrained anger is more hurtful to beholder than the injury that provokes it. Holding on to it is even worse. It is like grasping a hot coal, with the intent of throwing it at someone else; you are the one who gets burned. For, you are the first victim of your anger, and therefore it should be avoided not for the sake of moderation but for the sake of sanity.

Once you free yourself from hatred and anger, you will realise that regardless of the state of your life, you can change your situation or the way you think about it. Thus, you need to be true to yourself at all times. By embracing who you are and not who others want you to be, you open yourself up to the seventh heaven. For, your beauty lies in your authentic imperfections and your vulnerabilities. Hence, walk your path confidently and do not expect everyone to understand your journey. Importantly, do not let the opinions of others interfere with your reality. For, your ability to achieve your (life) goals is not a function of what others think of you. You are the architect of your destiny. Let your mistakes educate you, as you are powerful when you know you can fall down, pick yourself up, and move forward without seeking external approval – see Chapter 10. Therefore, shed-off that mask, because the people worth impressing would appreciate your authentic self. Besides, it is better to be disliked for who you are than being loved for who you are not. In a nutshell, by being yourself, you put something unique on earth; for the benefit of *the Fortress in a once Seemingly Peaceful Realm*.

Each time take a pace and steps that are suitable for you as you are not in a competition. Flowing from the foregoing therefore, do not waste your time comparing yourself with others. Just accept the reality of nature that each human being is unique in his own way. In fact, everything has its own identity, which is unsurpassable in the efficient functioning of the universe. So, do not try to be better than anybody else. Instead, strive to be better than the way you were yesterday by doing your best. If all Africans adopt this principle, *The Hate-spewing Ruffians, The Blood-sucking Urchins* and *The Violence-spitting Vipers* will have no place to hide in *the Fortress in a Seemingly Peaceful Realm*.

Unfortunately, in our modern world inundated with false shows where people are hated for being real, and loved for being fake, everyone wants to get to the top of the mountain first and shout: *Look at me! Look at my look!* However, the truth is, happiness and growth happen during the climbing and not while sitting at the peak. For this to happen though, you have to pay attention to each step. Otherwise, you will miss the magnificent view of life that comes from climbing the mountain – see also Chapter 1. For, *there* is no better than *here*.

'There' versus 'here'

The view's gorgeous where'er you stand.
As, 'there' is no better than 'here'.
When your 'there' becomes a 'here',
You attain a new 'there';
That'll, again, look better than 'here'.
For, 'here' is real while 'there' is a mirage.
Do not rush to reach the summit first,
For the view's glorious 'n life's joyous 'here' not 'there'.

Of primary importance, do not concern yourself with where others are in their climbing endeavour. Climb at your own rate and do not be rattled if other climbers pass you along the way. For, the process of climbing and growing is the source of your greatest benefits. In fact, if unable to climb up the mountain of life, sit and enjoy the valley by singing your song.

Sing your song

O' man!
When too weak to journey-up the mountain-of-life;
Sit in the valley 'n chant in happy measure.
As multitudes lazily pass along;
Though they may forget the singer,
They'll ne'er forget the song.
O' mine man!
Sing your song.
Dance your dance;
And, reach for your seventh heaven.

It does not matter therefore, how many times you fall or how messy your journey is, so long as you do not stop taking your bold baby steps forward. The Japanese understand this principle best. They call it *kaizen*. For lack of a better equivalent in English, it implies constant, gradual and simple improvements. The idea being that miniscule refinements consistently made result in compounded advancements at all levels. The more I experienced the effect of *kaizen* in my traditional martial arts training, the quicker I realized that it is an organizing principle capable of making a tremendous impact in one's entire life. My commitment to constantly improve and endlessly raise my standards in life has kept me both happy and successful.

Live in the now

Life is like a day at the beach - there is the sunburn, the scratchy sand in the pants, hot sand and probably rowdy beach-lovers. It all depends on how you look at it. Look for the negative things, and your day at the beach is spoilt. Look at the positive elements, and you have a marvellous experience.

To drive my point home, I share a true but alien sounding story, at least to those who have never been to the Arctic Circle. In January 2013, I had an opportunity to experience the annual return of the sun while on a visit to Inuvik town in Northwest Territories, Canada. For your information and future reference, the sun completely disappears for six months preceding the frigid winter season – marked by an average temperature of thirty-six Degrees Celsius below zero (-36^0C). People, both locals and (international) tourists, gather to witness this spectacular natural happening. That year, the first sliver of sun was expected to light-up the Arctic on a Sunday at 01:40 PM local time. The entire event normally lasts for about five minutes. Thereafter, the duration of sunlight increases each day until the region gets 24 hours of sunlight daily for six months straight.

I joined hundreds of other participants to witness this unique astronomical phenomenon. As crowds of people gathered at the pre-arranged viewing site, I entertained myself by watching the diversity of people coming to share the occasion. Enthusiasts had flown in from all corners of the world, at a cost of several thousands of dollars, to bear witness to an occurrence that would last not more than five minutes. To paraphrase one devotee, *we are not here to see a mere sunrise, but a re-birth of sunshine that will redeem us from darkness.*

At 01:36 PM, the cosmic-induced drama started to unfold. A palpable air of anxiety filled the atmosphere - anticipation of seeing the sun rise and indeed fear of disappointment. By 01:41 PM, a frail sun ray appeared in the horizon. We greeted it with excited applause – joyously danced with our hearts full of bliss. But soon the clouds rolled back, obscuring our view nearing the moment of absolute darkness. It became obvious, at least to some in the crowd, that we would not experience the re-birth of sunshine. As a social scientist, the way people dealt with their expectations intrigued me to a great extent. Each of them responded according to their rules on what needed to happen in order for their experience to be both fulfilling and memorable. An old man behind me cursed: [multiple expletive F-words], *I wasted my twenty-five thousand dollars for this damn thing?* A woman in front of me said unceasingly: *I cannot believe we have missed the whole* [expletive F-word] *thing...* The young lady on my right side excitedly ejaculated: *This is a life time experience. It is happening! Absolutely orgasmic! So happy to be here!* At the same time and with similar gusto, a middle-aged man standing at the far-front smashed his evidently expensive camcorder against a wall. Together with many others, he hurriedly returned to his hotel room to watch the annual phenomenon on television, just like everyone else across the globe.

A few minutes later, a dramatic thing happened – a bright sliver of sunlight re-appeared, getting brighter by the second. There was a roar through the remaining crowd, and almost as soon as it had begun, the re-birth of sunshine was over. In a near perfect fashion, the entire crowd hastily left the viewing scene. Most of them complained how they spent so much money, travelled long distances and now they have missed-out on a lifetime experience. Ironically, the sunrise was revealed for everyone to see, but few people remained to experience it. Worse even, only a few of those who remained enjoyed the excitement. Their minds were elsewhere – *'there'* and not *'here'*. Metaphorically, they continued to bang their fragile heads on the wall because of their unmet expectations for immediate gratification – see also Chapter 10.

This puzzled me profoundly. For me, the most remarkable moment of the event was the instant that a thin feeble sliver of the sun slipped out from the horizon, instantly bringing daylight with it. It occurred to me that not even the deepest darkness can stand against a ray of light. I equate that ray of light to a ray of love. A ray capable of melting the myriad forms of darkness that we encounter daily – remember the alphabet soup of vices listed in Chapter 2? For, love is the mother of all values– see also Chapter 10. It neutralizes hatred, egotism, negative ethnicity, violence, and any combination thereof. It has the power to defeat the triple archenemies - *The Hate-spewing Ruffians*, *The Blood-sucking Urchins* and *The Violence-spitting Vipers* – currently ravaging *the Fortress in a Seemingly Peaceful Realm*.

Let me take this experience a notch higher by examining it from a philosophical viewpoint. Does it shock you that people would pay a fortune, get so excited and emotional about a mere five-minute sunrise? How different is it from sun rising from the east every morning? What will happen if every day people in the world wake-up early to watch the sun rise? What makes us behave in such a robotic way? Response: we are the only animal species that take life miracles for granted. Our short-sighted egoistic rules crave for rarity at the expense of ordinary miracles. For we live *there* and not *here* and our *fabricated reality* has nothing to do with *true reality* - remember Ms. *Kunguru*'s story at the beginning of this chapter? This *artificial reality* is designed and interpreted through the controlling force of our bloated egos. Consequently, the grass is ever greener in the other side of the fence as we fail to grasp the simple but powerful truth that the *here* and *now* is what is important in life. Unsurprisingly, as pointed-out in Chapter 8, one only need to free himself from his muddled ego to have a clear view of things in order to appreciate real-life.

I complicate this further by asking you: who do you think had the worst experience during the sunrise event? Undoubtedly, those who had the most rigid expectations on what must happen before they could enjoy the moment. Of course, there is absolutely nothing wrong with having expectations in life. But, the argument here is that you need to live in the present – *here* and not *there*. You need to appreciate who you are and what you have at any given moment. If you are on the beach, prepare for the sunburn, be ready to have scratchy sand in your pants and embrace the rowdy beach-goers. Combined, these are elements that constitute a genuine beach tourism experience. They are so integral to beach activity that, without them, the activity loses its basic character and appeal. Further, if you are climbing a mountain, do not rush to reach the summit first, for the view is glorious and life is joyous wherever you are. This is what I call *authentic reality* or *real reality*.

With this frame of mind, I thoroughly enjoyed the sunrise in Inuvik for I had a pragmatic rule - to relish the event no matter what happened. By so doing, I committed to be intelligent, flexible and creative enough to direct my evaluations in a way that allowed me to experience the true richness of life. Probably, this should be the ultimate rule in *the Fortress in a Seemingly Peaceful Realm*.

Concluding remarks

Reflect on your achievement and give thanks to your allies, for they are your inspiration. Give thanks to your adversaries, for they are your teachers; to difficult people in your life, for they have shown you exactly who you do not want to be. To all the highs and lows, the twists and turns, for each has been a profound lesson. And, in-keeping with the foregoing, I say…

CHAPTER 12

Thank You Dear Reader: Concluding Remarks

Thank you!

Asante!
Dank je!
Grand merci!
Arigatō gozai-mashita!
Tremendous thanks!
For accompanyin' me through this journey.
Journey beyond negative ethnicity, corruption 'n violence.

Wish you happiness!
Remember though: happiness' a fabrication.
If you sow a seed of exultation;
Expect a seedlin' of elation.
If you water a seedlin' of elation;
Expect a tree of joy.
If you feed from a tree of joy;
Expect to be joyful.
Expect happiness dear reader!

As you pursue happiness,
Remember: happiness' about humility;
About love 'n fairness.
About self-denial of egotistical eccentric manipulations,
Of mass hysteria.
For, it ushers us to the magical world of simplicity 'n soulfulness.
Seek that kind of happiness!

Preamble

Let me start this last phase of our journey by re-telling an interesting story. This is a bout a fellow in London after World War II. He is sitting with a parcel wrapped in old newspapers on his lap. It is a rusty, huge and seemingly heavy object. The bus conductor comes up to him and asks: *What do you have on your lap, Sir?* And, the man answers: *It is an unexploded bomb. I dug it out of my garden; and, I am now taking it to the police station.* The conductor retorts: *Okay. It is better you do not carry it on your lap. Put it under your seat.*

What a solution! Transfer unexploded bomb from your lap to under your seat. Is that not exchanging a problem with another problem? Africa should avoid such a situation as she fights *The Hate-spewing Ruffians*, *The Blood-sucking Urchins* and *The Violence-spitting Vipers*.

Ripples of positive effects

What do you suppose is the common thread in the top-three monsters facing *the Fortress in a Seemingly Peaceful Realm* today? From negative ethnicity and corruption to violence, the response is that the root of these problems is a set of human behaviour.

Negative ethnicity is not a result of a viral infection; it is the consequence of a malignant behaviour. Corruption is not a bacteria-related malady; it is a behavioural degeneration. Even violence is not a biological malfunction; rather, it is a behavioural disintegration. These monsters are the off-spring of actions that Africans, individually and collectively, chose to take or not to take. Subsequently, the solution lies in the modification of the existent behaviours.

Flowing from above therefore, there are positive actions that all Africans can take in their homes; their businesses; and, in their communities that will initiate ripples of positive effects. For, through actions, human beings express their values. Then, the media expose such actions thereby, directly or indirectly, inciting other compatriots to take similar steps.

I can hear doubting-thomases vivaciously protest: *what can one person do to change a nation leave alone a continent?* Virtually anything. The only limit to your impact is your imagination and commitment – see also Chapter 7. You only need to have an extraordinary level of commitment and consistently do little things extraordinarily well. For, we all have the inborn capacity to take daring, courageous and noble steps to make life better for others, even when in the short-term it seems to be at our own expense. The capacity to do the right thing, to dare take a stand against, *The Hate-spewing Ruffians, The Blood-sucking Urchins* and *The Violence-spitting Vipers* is within you lovely reader.

The Fortress in a Seemingly Peaceful Realm: A sphere of unity

Africans have been unceasingly blowing air into their hot-air balloon. The balloon became bigger and impressive. Historians zealously recorded the key milestones: when Africans invented an efficient way to inflate it; when they found marvellous chemicals that boosted its stretchability; when it attained certain sizes; and, how smoothly it glided through the sky. All these are important achievements. But, none was as pertinent as when the first rupture appeared in its skin - starting with a minute hole, and then air profusely whistled-out. That date is when Africans gave *The Hate-spewing Ruffians, The Blood-sucking Urchins* and *The Violence-spitting Vipers* a cart-blanche to rule *the Fortress in a Seemingly Peaceful Realm*. That is a date indelibly marked by heinous acts of: negative ethnicity, corruption and violence – see for example chapters 2, 4, 5 and 7.

Now it is time to mend the ruptured hot-air balloon, to unite and shape the destiny of *the Fortress*. The collective action against these three known challenges will determine the quality of life for future generations. Importantly, Africans should avoid getting fixated on what is not working, which will limit their focus to effects and not the causes of the problems. In such a situation, people fail to recognize that, it is the small actions taken daily that create the preferred destiny – remember the concept of *kaizen* described in Chapter 11? For life is cumulative; and, the ocean will be less without a drop.

Leading from above therefore, the situation Africa is experiencing is the accumulation of a host of actions citizens have (not) taken as individuals, as families and as communities. For, the success or failure of a nation is usually not the result of one cataclysmic event, although sometimes it may look that way. Rather, it results from the actions taken day-in, day-out. Therefore, it rests upon each African to take responsibility on an individual level just like the little *Kolibri* in Chapter 4. Ultimately, that will make the difference whether Africa will free herself from the three senseless monsters and their ugly siblings. Against this background, it is easy to deduce that in order to bring about positive changes in the joint destiny, Africa has to embrace the concept of equal opportunities; nurture good leadership; and, re-submit herself to pure love – see chapters 3, 8 and 9. Only then can *the Fortress in a Seemingly Peaceful Realm* be free from *The Hate-spewing Ruffians* - negative ethnicity.

Negative ethnicity: *The Hate-spewing Ruffians*

Beyond this book is the outraged conscience of a continent and the harsh judgment of history on her people's actions and/or inactions. No one should be denied the possibility to participate in national building. This can be ensured by treating everyone equally – see for example Chapter 3. At the basic level, equal opportunity bestows dignity to humanity as it is insensitive to one's possessions and appearance. It rests on one's right to be treated as equal among others and enables one to live in accordance to his ability and merits. African countries therefore need to overcome the crippling legacy of favouritism. Once done, it will brighten the lives of all.

Further, to eliminate mistrust and suspicion amongst ethnic groupings in *the Fortress in a Seemingly Peaceful Realm*, Africans need to deal with one another in a sincere and honest manner – see Chapter 2. They must say openly to each other the things they hold in their hearts; things too often said only behind closed doors. There must be a sustained effort to listen to each other, to learn from each other, to respect one another, and to seek common ground. For in diversity, broadly defined, there is beauty and strength.

Once you embrace Africa's diversity, you automatically realize that it does not matter whether you are a 'rose' or a 'water-lilly' or a 'bristle-grass' – Chapter 3. What matters is that you are flowering. Embrace it! Be proud of it, as everything has beauty. Thus, I invite all Africans to *The Perspective-Changing Club; The Club of Love*. I invite Africans to see and appreciate that beauty for that is what makes *the Fortress in a Seemingly Peaceful Realm* unique and beautiful; strong and lovely.

Evidently, the foregoing takes will and mental effort. Some days you would not be able to do it, or you just flat-out would not want to do it. And, that is fine. But, choose to look differently at that mean-eyed, unkempt father who has just yelled at his little son in a soccer practice – maybe he is not usually like that; maybe he has been up three straight nights holding the hand of his dear wife who is bedridden with breast cancer. Of course, I exaggerate just a bit.

Anyhow, the point is: when human beings operate on their default-setting, they never consider possibilities that are not obvious. Conversely, if love and compassion drive their lives, they learn to pay attention to other options. It enables them to empathise with those whose reality differs from theirs. It gives them the impetus to venture outside the bounds of their realms and ponder how it would feel to have been born other than the way they are. Eventually, they hear the screams of others; and, open hearts to their sufferings. This is the only sure way to defeat *The Hate-spewing Ruffians* attacking *the Fortress in a Seemingly Peaceful Realm*.

This is the most effective solution to negative ethnicity across Africa. Further, once Africans combine love with the principles of equal opportunities and good leadership, *the Fortress* will triumph over *The Blood-sucking Urchins* - corruption.

Corruption: *The Blood-sucking Urchins*

Heightened productivity gives rise to four benefits. Firstly, as individuals control what they produce and consume, their lives improve. Secondly, when citizens are economically empowered, institutions are forced to become more responsive to their needs.

Thirdly, by becoming more productive, consumers are able to pay for productivity tools, creating opportunities for entrepreneurs to launch profit-seeking enterprises to provide such tools. This is how and why businesses selling computers and cellular phones and related services sprang up effortlessly throughout Africa. Fourthly, successful businesses attract competition. Fair competition gives rise to innovation, specialization, scalability, lower prices and higher wages. It is unstoppable self-propelling cycle of organic economic growth capable of reinvigorating any society.

The moment all corners of Africa enjoy these four benefits, then, *The Blood-sucking Urchins* will no longer fly in the skies of *the Fortress in a Seemingly Peaceful Realm*. And, Africans will enjoy true fruits of their labour as corruption will be a thing of the past – Chapter 4.

And, again, once equal opportunities-good leadership-love nexus is operationalised, Africa will automatically be a continent without *The Violence-spitting Vipers* - violence.

Violence: *The Violence-spitting Vipers*

To make what seems impossible possible, each African should fight for his seat at the table. Better even, every African should fight for a seat at the head of the table as that is what he deserves. Ceaselessly, fight for your opportunity to pursue and achieve your dreams. As you do so though, keep your flag of peace flying; your trumpet of unity sounding; and, your bells of love ringing.

Consequently, Africans must move past indecision to action. For, if they do not act, they shall be dragged down the twisted, dark and shameful corridors that are reserved for those who possess power without compassion; might without morality; and, strength without sight. Citizens should therefore, never look with prideful righteousness on the troubles of their neighbours.

Everyone should enjoy a violence-free life, as violence in its very nature strikes from one's hands the very weapons which he seeks – progress and belief in his values. It leaves everyone standing bare, naked and dejected with a lost opportunity. Once Africans replace egotism with modesty; arrogance with humility; hatred with love; and, violence with peace, they will have dealt an overwhelming blow to *The Violence-spitting Vipers* presently devastating *the Fortress in a Seemingly Peaceful Realm*. They will have freed Africa of domestic as well as political violence.

Undivided love: antidote to the three monsters

Before bringing this journey to a close, I feel impelled to mention that Africa remains a living, breathing organism imperilled by the sickness of negative ethnicity, the disease of corruption, and the malady of violence. Consequently, if her soul becomes wholly poisoned, the autopsy must read both unequivocally and distinctly: negative ethnicity, corruption and violence. For, ethnic-profiling is omnipresent in all aspects of lives; corruption suffocates the highest to the lowest public/private offices; and, violence is a defining characteristic in homes and streets. As a result, aimlessness among the youth; anxiety among the elders; and, virtual despair among the many who look beyond material success for the inner meaning of their lives are discernible.

Unashamedly, those who would trade their African brotherhood for the gravy train of these vices tend to believe in a utopian universe of peace without victory. To them, if Africans avoid any direct confrontation with the enemy, he will forget his evil ways and learn to love them. Anyone who opposes this distorted solution is indicted as offering knee-jerk solutions to complex problems. The bottom line remains however, no African should make a deal with these fugly slave masters – negative ethnicity, corruption and violence.

For life is so dear to be purchased at the price of chains and slavery. If nothing in life is worth dying for, when did this begin - just in the face of these tripartite enemies? Or, should Africa's freedom fighters have thrown down their guns and refused to fire the shots heard around the world half a century ago? Did those who died did so in vain? Where, then, is the road to a peaceful and prosperous Africa? It is a simple answer after all.

That answer lies in Africa's ability to tell these monsters: *There is a price I will not pay; there is a point beyond which you must not advance.* Only then, Africans will be able to preserve for their children the best of *the Fortress in a Seemingly Peaceful Realm*. Consequently, Africans must go forth from here united, determined as there is no substitute for victory against these priority monsters: *The Hate-spewing Ruffians, The Blood-sucking Urchins* and *The Violence-spitting Vipers*; victory over these vices: negative ethnicity, corruption and violence.

Ultimately, the true antidote to negative ethnicity, corruption, violence and their related ugliness is undivided love – as discussed in Chapter 9. Just like the rising sun dispels the darkness of the night, genuine love banishes the darkness of selfishness and hatred from one's heart. Drink from the chalice of real love and save *the Fortress in a Seemingly Peaceful Realm* from ethnic vanity.

However, while each of these four tools – good leadership; love; accepting failure; and, gratitude –, on its own is capable of dealing a deadly blow on these marauding monsters, under the right conditions, they are most effective when used together. Once negative ethnicity is defeated, corruption is eliminated and violence is conquered, then Africa will change both in the short- and in the long-term. This modest book serves as a step, albeit a small one, towards that direction and destination. Destination *Beyond Negative Ethnicity, Corruption and Violence*.

PARTING WORDS

I am convinced that if Africans are to get to the right side of history, they as a people must undergo a radical revolution of values. They must rapidly shift from a material-obsessed to a value-oriented society. When profit motives and property rights are considered more important than people, the giant triplets of negative ethnicity, corruption and violence will remain unconquered. They will remain free to roam and spread hatred, bigotry, violence and socio-economic callousness in *the Fortress in a Seemingly Peaceful Realm*.

In a world fixated with material gains, pessimism and cynicism set in. People become numb to acts of violence. Thus, violence no longer surprises them, and instead, they are surprised by spontaneous acts of compassion; unrewarded gestures of kindness; and, courageous movements of unity and love.

Conversely, in a value-driven society, people embrace the constant flux of the universe. They perceive all vantage points; listen to all stories; and, remain open to multiple realities. In darkness, they are guided by intuition; in weakness, they use humility as their spear; and, in fear, they use love as their shield. With that in mind, I conclude our journey, *Beyond Negative Ethnicity, Corruption and Violence*, by challenging you dear reader, to be an excellent example.

Be an excellent example

Dear reader,
Live life fully.
Take care of yourself.
Of all the paths you take in life,
Make sure a few of them are dirt.
Have fun 'n be crazy.
Go out 'n screw up.
And, enjoy the process.

Don't be trapp'd by dogma;
Don't allow your inner voice be drown'd by others' opinions.
Have the courage to follow your intuitions.
Don't let people pull you into their storms;
Instead, pull them into your peace.

Learn from your mistakes;
Without tryin' to be perfect.
Just be an excellent example.
Be a champion of goodness 'n the dispossess'd.
Don't lose the power of spontaneity;
The pleasure that comes from being silly...
And, being like a child.
As you venture beyond negative ethnicity, corruption 'n violence.

REFERENCES

Bible, the
Home Office – UK (1995) *The 1995 Home Office Research Study in England and Wales.* London, UK.
Kibicho, W. (2016) *Traditional Martial Arts: A Portrait of a Living Art.* Ottawa: Sakata Publishers.
King, M.L. (Jnr.) Speeches (Courtesy of Martin Luther King Jnr Centre, Atlanta, Georgia).
Knight, C. and Stemplowska, Z. (eds.) (2011) *Responsibility and Distributive Justice.* Oxford: Oxford University Press.
Mandela, N. (1995) *Long Walk to Freedom.* South Africa: Little Brown & Company.
Mello, A. (de) (1990) *Awareness: the Perils and Opportunities of Reality.* New York: Doubleday
Musashi, M. (1974) *A Book of Five Rings: The Classic Guide to Strategy.* New York: The Overlook Press.
Statistics Canada (2000) *The Canadian General Social Survey.* Government of Canada: Ottawa
Statistics Canada (2005) *The Canadian General Social Survey.* Government of Canada: Ottawa.
Straus, M. and Gelles, R. (1975) *The U.S. National Family Violence Survey.* Washington, D.C., United States.
USA, Government of the, (1990) *The National Comorbidity Survey.* Washington, D.C., United States.
Wood, M., Maltby, J., Stewart, N., & Joseph, S. (2008). "Conceptualizing Gratitude and Appreciation as a Unitary Personality Trait." *Personality and Individual Differences,* 44, 619–630.

APPENDICES

Appendix 1: Definitions of some terms as used in the text

Attack season: Any day of the year while the 'night' is the electioneering year.

Arch-shooting Squadron, the: The police services in the continent.

Blood-sucking Urchin, the: Corruption of all kinds while *The Blood-sucking Urchins* are the corrupt individuals.

Bunyot: Kalenjin term for traitor

Chama: Kiswahili term for informal savings group. It is a social organization formed to help members save money for specific purposes, either at individual or community level. Rotating Savings is the most common in rural Kenya.

Corruption: Dishonest or fraudulent illegal conduct by those in positions of authority or power.

Domestic violence (DV): Violence that takes place in the home, especially by one person against their partner.

Economic rent: Economic rent arises when an individual possess something of unique value. Such possession can be a plot of land in the central business district of a city or a piece of land where an oil well has been discovered. The owner of such an asset can charge an arbitrary price for its use.

Equal opportunity: State in which everyone is equal, especially in status, rights, and socio-economic and political opportunities.

Fortress in a Seemingly Peaceful Realm, the: the continent of Africa.

Gratitude: Deeper appreciation for someone and/or something whether tangible or intangible, which produces longer lasting positivity.

Hate-spewing Ruffian, the: Negative ethnicity while *The Hate-spewing Ruffians* are ethnic chauvinists.

HIV/AIDS: Human Immunodeficiency Virus (HIV) is the virus that can cause *Acquired Immune Deficiency Syndrome* (AIDS). HIV infects humans and causes damage by taking over cells in the immune system - the part of the body that fights off germs, bacteria and disease. When that happens, the body is unable to fight off certain types of illnesses. Once the immune system is damaged to a certain level, the person is diagnosed with AIDS.

Kaizen: Japanese term that implies constant, gradual and simple improvements.

Kayamba: A raft rattle idiophone from East Africa. It contains seeds or small pebbles between two trays or rafts made from numerous lengths of cane tied together. The two rafts are separated from one another by slats of wood that form the sidewalls of the instrument.

Lance-launching Cavalry, the: The Judiciary and the offices of the public prosecution in Africa.

Leadership: Qualities that make someone a good leader, or the methods a leader uses to realize his set goals.

Mwizi: Kiswahili term for thief.

Negative ethnicity: Belief that people of some ethnic background(s) are inferior to others, and the prejudicial behaviour which results from this belief. It is a degraded version of racism.

Night: The electioneering year in any country in Africa.

Prejudice: Unjustified and negative attitude towards an individual based solely on his membership to a certain social group.

Safari: Journey

Stereotype: Attributing some characteristics to a person that are assumed to be shared by members of a group. Thus, it assigns individuals to particular categories.

Violence-spitting Viper, the: Violence of all forms while *The Violence-spitting Vipers* are violent individuals or propagators of violence.

War Council, the: The Cabinet of any ruling government in Africa.

Waterball-slinging Platoon, the: The anti-corruption commissions/bodies and the electoral commissions/bodies in Africa.

Appendix 2: Countries visited during the field work

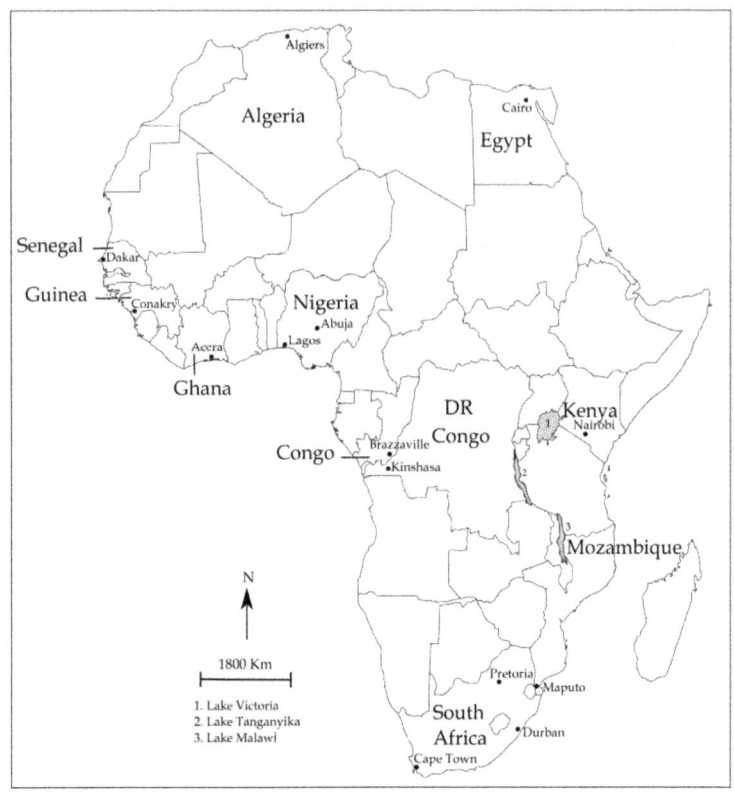

Appendix 3: Kenya's cities, national parks and reserves mentioned in the book

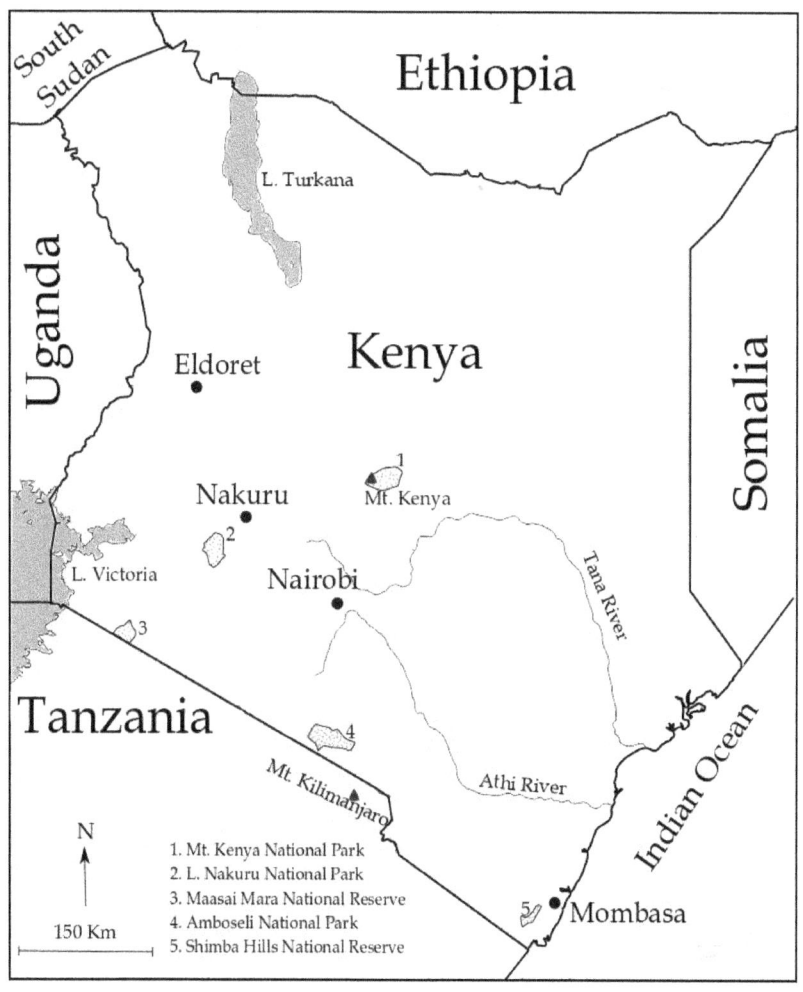

1. Mt. Kenya National Park
2. L. Nakuru National Park
3. Maasai Mara National Reserve
4. Amboseli National Park
5. Shimba Hills National Reserve

Appendix 4: First four letters after the 2008 attack to Isaac

Letter I

Dear Isaac,

I hope that you are better today than yesterday.

Thank you so much for sharing your story with me. Many thanks for your trust. I cannot tell you how proud I am that you let me in; that you have asked for help instead of trying to cope alone. For, a problem shared, is a problem half-solved.

I know it hurts and that everything seems dim, but, you are strong! The spark inside you is very much alive. I want you to know that there is a way through this, and you only need to belief in yourself.

You need to remain hopeful.
For, losing hope will cripple you;
Tie you to the past; and,
Keep your sight upon things beyond your influence.

I know you Isaac, and I know the warrior in you. You are a fighter. And, importantly, you are not alone on this. Please know that whatever measure of comfort I can provide, I will provide. Whatever portion of sadness that I can share with you to ease this heavy load, I will gladly bear it. Isaac, you are not alone!

Take good care of yourself Isaac.

Feel free to contact me anytime, if need be.

[**Signed and dated:** Saturday, 26th January 2008]

Letter II

Dear Isaac,

I trust this letter finds you as it leaves me, in good spirit.

Oftentimes, things happen to us;
Things we do not understand; and,
Things we cannot control.
They blind-side us; and,
Strip us to the core of who we are,
Leaving us raw and bleeding.

In that moment, when we feel like there is nothing left, it is then when we need to remember that we all have an inborn gift. A gift that no one can snatch from us. That gift is choice.

Isaac, you have the choice. It is only you, who can choose where your thoughts go - upon the anguish or upon the possibilities in your future.

You have the choice to keep walking forward;
Not to surrender to despair; and,
Not to drift-away and be lost in the void of your pain.

Have a good day Isaac.

[**Signed and dated:** Wednesday, 13th February 2008]

Letter III

Dear Isaac,

It is my sincere hope that you are all well.

As I told you a couple of days ago, you undeniably have a choice out of this mess dearest Isaac.

Give a thought of what I am telling you! Sure, the choice to move forward might seem onerous. But then, a gem cannot be polished without friction, nor can a man be perfected without trials.

Think about how empowering this is!
Let this power infuse you!
Let it pour liquid steel through your spine.
And, you will come out a winner!

Isaac, you have power!
You can fight!
You can win!
And, you shall win!

I wish you the very best Isaac;
And, share my unadulterated love with the rest of your family.

[Signed and dated: Thursday, 21st February 2008]

Letter IV

Dear Isaac,

I am happy to hear that you are doing better than last week. Brighter days are coming.

I am not saying that there won't be difficult times… But, who does not have up-and-down moments? It is only in our darkest hours that we discover the true strength of the brilliant light within ourselves that can never be dimmed.

To some, dark hours seem like endless desolate deserts. Nevertheless, trust me Isaac: there are abundant unexpected streams hidden in those barren places. They will see you through to the next greener stop. You only need to keep your head-up bearing in mind that the greatest glory in life lies not in never falling, but in rising every time we fall.

Isaac, you will beat this!
Problems are not stop signs;
They are guidelines.
In fact, every agony carries with it a seed,
A seed of a greater benefit.
Think of that seed and not the agony…
And, your load will be easier.

I wish you well dearest Isaac;

[**Signed and dated:** Tuesday, 18th March 2008]

ABOUT THE AUTHOR

Wanjohi Kibicho, Ph.D. has twenty years of university teaching experience. He has published widely on tourism management, sex tourism, sustainable tourism and traditional martial arts. Dr. Kibicho also does international consultancy in all aspects of the tourism industry. He is a perfervid traditional martial artist who stresses the benefits of the art towards body-mind-soul enlightenment.

He is an outspoken voice on issues of love-based cross-cultural understanding. He accordingly describes himself as hereunder:

I'm like a child who;
Loves wild flowers.
Loves smell of freshly mow'd grass.
A simple mortal who:
Trusts to be trust'd;
Loves to be lov'd.
A mere earthlin';
Made entirely of flaws.
Flaws stitch'd together;
But with good intentions.
For, I'm like a child without being a child.